KILEY
SESSION
#10
5-2010

1/1

A knowledge resource from The Masters Program

"A profound and prophetic book for such a time as this—for either we will find ways to unleash the energy, resources, and talents of our high-capacity marketplace leaders or we will see the church continue to be marginalized in its impact on the affairs of men and culture. *Unlimited Partnership* provides the blueprint for engaging the most-resourced group in the history of the world to reclaim the high ground for the Kingdom as agents for change and transformation. Imagine the impact of this unlimited potential unleashed by these 'holy' unlimited partnerships."

> **David Allman**—President of Regent Partners
> (using his skills partnering with his pastor,
> Andy Stanley; helping his church, Northpoint
> Community Church, to impact Atlanta
> and beyond)

"God has uniquely equipped Lloyd Reeb to be a thought leader in the emerging arena of leadership discovery. He is an expert in assisting churches and ministries in their efforts to discover and deploy seasoned leaders into service."

> **Bob Buford**—Author of
> *Halftime* and *Finishing Well*,
> Founder of Leadership Network

UNLIMITED
PARTNERSHIP

UNLIMITED
PARTNERSHIP

IGNITING A MARKETPLACE LEADER'S
JOURNEY TO SIGNIFICANCE

LLOYD REEB   BILL WELLONS

PUBLISHING GROUP

NASHVILLE, TENNESSEE

ISBN: 978-0-8054-4450-6

Published by B & H Publishing Group,
Nashville, Tennessee

Dewey: 253.7
Subject Heading: MINISTRY \ EVANGELISTIC WORK
                 CHURCH WORK WITH COMMUNITY

10 9 8 7 6 5 4 3 2 1   10 09 08 07 06

Contents

Author's Note

This unique flip book is intended to enable you and your pastor or ministry leader to partner together to change the world.

If you are a business or professional leader, read this side of the book, and give a copy of the book to your pastor to read the other side. Then take some time to look through the pastor's side of this book to get a glimpse inside how he is thinking and the issues he faces in this partnership.

FOREWORD

A growing number of seasoned business and professional leaders want to use their skills and experience to make a difference for the Lord in their world—and one obvious place for doing so is through their church. But many feel stuck. They have no idea where to begin or who to talk to.

At the same time, pastors and church leaders long for their churches to make an even greater impact for Christ in their communities and around the world, but they lack the seasoned leaders and ministry model necessary to make it happen.

What is desperately needed *now* is a way to join these two groups of people together to unleash the kingdom power that such a partnership can provide.

This unique book does that. Read it one direction to understand the perspective and challenges facing a pastor. Flip it over to comprehend the perspective and issues facing a business or professional leader. Both viewpoints have been written to bridge the gap and exploit the spiritual potential that exists between high-capacity leaders and kingdom-minded pastors (and parachurch leaders).

Whether you are a church leader or marketplace leader, let me invite you to read both viewpoints. Then you will be ready to develop a partnership with unlimited potential for spiritual influence. King Solomon, the wisest man ever to live, once said, "Two are better than one because they have a good return for their labor" (Eccles. 4:9 NASB). I believe you will find a new power of "two together" in the pages of this book.

Both sides of this partnership are practical and relevant, filled with compelling real-life stories of business and professional leaders and pastors who are connecting for the first time to make a leveraged impact for God's kingdom. These stories will not only inspire you; they will challenge you to the core.

People like this, who want to pursue significance in their second half of life, have come to be called Halftimers, and the Halftime movement is a growing phenomenon. It simply did not exist in previous generations. It is a new movement of God representing unprecedented opportunities for the church. Pastors, please don't miss this opportunity to empower and release these seasoned leaders in your church for greater kingdom impact. And Halftimers, please don't turn your back on the prompting of God in your heart to leverage your skills and experiences for eternal significance. There is a thrilling adventure out there for both of you when you are willing to trust God for this ministry partnership.

As founder and teaching pastor of a large church for more than thirty years, Bill Wellons has led the way by methodically finding and engaging Halftimers to serve both inside and outside his church. Having served with Bill personally, I know firsthand that he brings to his writing a host of proven practices from this wealth of experience.

As a successful real estate developer and business leader, Lloyd Reeb shares his own personal journey from success to significance. God is now using Lloyd as the national spokesperson for Halftime as well as the pastor of leadership development for his church. Lloyd uniquely brings the Halftimer's perspective to kingdom work, along with a sense of unwavering optimism for his peers.

These men long to help pastors and marketplace leaders lock arms as partners to courageously advance the kingdom of God together. Together is *always* better.

Dr. Robert M. Lewis
Author, *The Church of Irresistible Influence*
Founder of Men's Fraternity

CHAPTER 1

YOU ARE NOT ALONE

Chris Danzi met me in the lobby of our church. He'd heard how I had reoriented my life from focusing on success to pursuing significance, and he had some questions. "I wanted two things in life," he said over coffee. "I wanted to be senior VP at the bank, and I wanted a silver BMW. This year I got both of them," pointing out the window to his shiny new Beemer sitting just outside. "But I feel like the dog that finally caught the car. These two things have not satisfied me in the ways I thought they would." After a long pause he continued. "What's wrong with me? Am I having a midlife crisis?"

Sandy Griffith reached midlife and looked back over her first half, which had focused on raising and launching two well-balanced kids. "That was fun, and perhaps the most significant thing I will ever do, but what now? What do I do with the rest of my life?"

Many people reaching midlife have experienced some measure of success yet wonder what will make their second half significant. Most aren't financially independent—they can't quit their job—but they do have options about how they spend their time and talent. Chris cannot leave his role at the bank, and Sandy still has remaining family responsibilities, but both have options. You will discover in the many stories in this book that you do not have to leave your job to pursue significance in your second half of life.

Both Chris and Sandy created time and space in their lives by cutting out the clutter of low-value activities, enabling them to discover what they're most passionate about and to begin to make unique impacts. They found that their own church was a wonderful place to start.

I remember reaching a point in my real estate development career when I began to ask if there's more to life than this. Do I just keep building these buildings and accumulating more stuff, or is there something bigger and more meaningful that I can live for? I remember a moment when I looked up at one of the buildings my partner and I had just finished and realized that in one hundred years it would be torn down.

This stage of life has come to be known as Halftime—a pause in midlife to look back on all we have experienced (both successes and failures), what we've learned, and who we've become, and then to redirect our lives for the second half.

Both Chris and Sandy built a relationship with their pastor and began to explore opportunities for service that fit their skills and passions. Chris fell in love with the idea that he could make a difference in the lives of AIDS orphans in Africa. Sandy drew on her experience as a mom with a premature baby and felt a deep longing in her heart to hold, rock, and nurture preemie babies that no one seemed to care about.

Chris launched a brand-new ministry in his church designed to impact African villages most devastated by AIDS. "These com-

Chris Danzi

munities we serve have had an entire generation of parents wiped out by AIDS. There are almost no parents. I've had the privilege of growing a ministry that today provides food, clothing, education, and housing to more than five hundred boys and girls.

"These children are learning about the love and forgiveness of God through Jesus Christ, and they simply would not have if we hadn't shown up. Frankly, I'm blown away that God can use an ordinary banker like me to make this kind of eternal impact in these children's lives—and we have only just begun."

Every Friday morning you'll find Sandy in the Level 2, High Risk nursery unit of Houston's Ben Taub Hospital. Sitting in a circle of rocking chairs donated by her church, this forty-four-year-old mother of two rocks, feeds, soothes and, most importantly, prays, asking God to bless these premature infants and those struggling to overcome other severe health problems.

Today, other moms are volunteering as part of her ministry. The hospital invited her pastor to help dedicate the opening of an entire apartment suite inside the hospital to help the young mothers of the babies cared for by Sandy's ministry.

Fifteen years ago, Sandy held her own premature son. "I was able to be there with him the entire time he was in intensive care. While I held him, I looked around the room and realized there

Sandy Griffith

were ten other babies, but my son was the only baby held for any length of time. As I held my son, I promised God I was going to rock and hold babies for mothers who can't be there."

Eight years later Sandy began holding, feeding, and blessing the premature babies of fourteen-year-old mothers, crack addicts, and the working poor. "I came to Ben Taub Hospital to fill my arms, to give love," Sandy confesses, "but I'm the one who has been showered with love. I couldn't be in a more blessed situation."

A New Day

For the first time in human history, a growing number of us who reach midlife have the flexibility to reallocate part of our time and resources toward serving others. That might be in our marketplace environment, in our church or community, or even globally. Today when we reach midlife, we have the opportunity to stop, listen to God, and refocus our life around the skills and passions that have emerged in our first half. We have the chance to live the life of impact and adventure that Sandy and Chris are living.

This is a brand-new phenomenon that previous generations simply didn't enjoy. Three factors have combined to create this new opportunity for us:

1. *Longevity*—The average life expectancy only a hundred years ago was forty-seven years. Today when we reach fifty, we have thirty bonus years.

2. *Resources*—This is the healthiest, wealthiest, and best-educated generation in North America to ever reach midlife.

3. *Our desire to change the world*—When we look back, we remember that in our youth we had dreams of changing the world; and then we got caught up in the aspirations, busyness, and responsibilities of life.

The late Peter Drucker, the father of modern management,[1] said, "In a few hundred years, when the history of our time will be written from a long-term perspective, it is likely that the most important event historians will see is not technology, not the internet, not e-commerce. It is an unprecedented change in the human condition. For the first time—literally—substantial and rapidly growing numbers of people have choices. For the first time, they will have to manage themselves. And society is totally unprepared for it."

Peter Drucker's observations and the stories of Chris and Sandy may have just put words to what you are feeling in your own heart—a longing to move from success to significance. If so, then you're about to launch out on a journey that may be new in human history, but you are not alone. Thousands all around you are on this journey. In this book Bill Wellons and I have captured some of the most compelling stories from the journey we've come across. We also have reviewed the process others have gone through, to help you find your way.

While this social phenomenon called Halftime is unprecedented, it is *not* the first time in human history that a wave of Christians have had the opportunity to step up to the plate to change the course of history. Perhaps the greatest social movement of all time occurred during the Roman Empire, as the fledgling church of Jesus began to flourish. Long before the longevity, affluence, and opportunity to pursue significance that we enjoy even existed, Christians partnered with their church to make a difference in their community—and it led to the social movement known as the "rise of Christianity."

The overwhelming success of this movement raises a great question. As sociologist Rodney Stark puts it, "How did a tiny and obscure messianic movement from the edge of the Roman Empire dislodge classical paganism and become the dominant faith of Western Civilization?"[2] How was this possible? The consensus among a variety of church sources is that Christians were able to make a huge impact because they were so thoroughly committed to living out their faith in all areas of their lives. It is these transformed lives and the lifestyles they lived in the face of great difficulty under Roman rule that mark their social movement as the greatest.

As in our day, there were macro social and economic factors that made the movement possible. The Roman Empire had established peace, roads, common language, and other such factors that aided the spread of Christianity. In addition, most historians agree that early persecution of Christians actually benefited the rise of Christianity. Without persecution, the members of the first church might have stayed in Jerusalem indefinitely. As Tertullian once said, "The blood of the martyrs is the seed of the church."

But when the second great health epidemic struck the Roman world around AD 260, it provided a challenging backdrop against which Christianity as a social movement proved its mettle. At its height, five thousand people a day were reported to have died in the city of Rome alone.[3] How did the growing *multitude* of Christians respond at this unique *moment* in history? What was their common *mission,* and how did it add greater *meaning* and a sense of purpose to their lives?

Acknowledging the enormous death rate, Dionysius, bishop of Alexandria, wrote a lengthy tribute to the heroic nursing efforts of local Christians, many of whom lost their lives caring for others during this epidemic.

> Most of our brother Christians showed unbounded love and loyalty, never sparing themselves and thinking only of one another. Heedless of danger, they took charge of the sick, attending to their every need and ministering to them in Christ, and with them departed this life serenely happy; for they were infected by others with the disease, drawing on themselves the sickness of their neighbors and cheerfully accepting their pains. Many, in nursing and curing others, transferred their death to themselves and died in their stead. . . . The best of our brothers lost their lives in this manner, a number of presbyters, deacons, and laymen winning high commendation so that death in this form, the result of great piety and strong faith, seems in every way the equal of martyrdom.[4]

At a time when pagan faiths were found lacking, Christianity offered explanation and comfort. More importantly, Christian doctrine provided a prescription for action: "It is more blessed to give than to receive." This was radical thinking in a pagan world. Christians wanted to serve others by showing compassion for them because this is how God had loved them. "For while we were still helpless, at the right time Christ died for the ungodly" (Rom. 5:6).

Evidence even from pagan sources confirms that this was characteristic Christian behavior. It was a shining moment for the church. A century later the emperor Julian, who loathed Christians, launched a campaign to institute pagan charities to match the Christians. He complained in a letter to the high priest of Galatia in AD 362 that the pagans needed to somehow equal the virtues of Christians, for recent Christian growth was caused by their "moral character, even if pretended," and by their "benevolence toward strangers and care for the graves of the dead." He also wrote, "The impious Galileans support not only their poor, but ours as well, everyone can see that our people lack aid from us."[5]

Karen Jo Torjesen, dean of the School of Religion at Claremont Graduate University in California, recently weighed in on this issue. As "a historian of the period, I will leave to others the task of discerning what might be relevant now," Karen e-mailed my mentor, Bob Buford. Torjesen suggests that Christianity became a foundation for a new society.

> Converts who join the Christian churches in the third century are joining a new society. The clergy are their rulers, they are part of a social body that is providing care for orphans, for the sick, help for travelers, clothing for the poor, food for prisoners, burial grounds for those who need it. The churches have catechetical schools, libraries, rites of initiation, storehouses for liturgical equipment, ceremonies of ordination, specialized offices like healer, exorcist, teacher, widow and virgin. In fact it has more social services than the city, along with an effective administrative structure for delivering those services. In sum it is the Roman administrative genius added to the vision of the church as a family where the family has become a small city.[6]

Simply stated, this social movement was generating unthinkable changes in values and ways of life in Rome. Christians were penetrating the world with the love of Christ by living out what they claimed they believed.

A New Movement

Today, you, too, can be part of a new social movement. We believe that a social movement is best defined as a *multitude* of people at a unique *moment* in history with a common *mission* who experience greater *meaning* in their lives. During the rise of Christianity, a small group of Christians had the privilege of spawning a revolution that grew exponentially in only four hundred years.

Here's what it looked like:

A multitude of people—An estimated six million Christians by the year AD 300 grew to more than thirty-three million in only fifty years, according to sociologist Rodney Stark.[7]

Living at a unique moment in history—the first three hundred to four hundred years after the death and resurrection of Jesus Christ, when the circumstances under Roman rule made this rapid growth possible.

With a common mission—to penetrate the world with the sacrificial love of Christ. Christians wanted to please their God by serving the needs of others in the manner that they had been served by their Savior. "For even the Son of Man did not come to be served, but to serve, and to give His life a ransom for many" (Mark 10:45 NASB). There were no models in their culture for this kind of radical love in action.

Experiencing greater meaning in their lives. These Christ-followers enjoyed the privilege of partnering with God. They gave their lives to benefit others, and it felt significant to them because it *was* significant. Their lives had a clear purpose—and it was not about them.

Today more than twelve thousand people turn fifty every day in America. According to a study by Harvard and MetLife, half of all Americans aged fifty to seventy are interested in working to help the poor, elderly, and other people in need. The focus of these people in finding a second career or second-half focus is to stay involved with other people, find a sense of purpose, and help improve the quality of life in their community.

Another recent survey by MetLife Foundation and Civic Ventures, called "The New Face of Work" (April 2005), constitutes the first in-depth look at the pre-boomers and leading-edge boomers' priorities for the next stage of work. Questions explored in their research included:

- What kind of work does the current and coming generation of Americans in their fifties and sixties actually want to do?
- What are these individuals looking to accomplish through work after the traditional working years?
- Do these priorities fit with where we are likely to need people?
- Is there a great disjuncture between what the new generation of aging workers wants and what the economy and society need?

They found that most of us want to make a difference with our second half. The summary facts of the survey are:

1. *Half of all Americans age fifty to seventy want work that helps others.* A full 50 percent are interested in taking jobs now and in retirement that help improve the quality of life in their communities. What kind of work do they want to do?

- More than three-quarters (78 percent) are interested in working to help the poor, the elderly, and other people in need.
- Fifty-six percent are interested in dealing with health issues, whether working in a hospital or with an organization fighting a particular disease.
- Fifty-five percent are interested in teaching or other educational positions.
- Forty-five percent say they are interested in working in a youth program.[8]

2. *Second careers in the retirement years are about people, purpose, and community.* When specifically asked "Why do you

(Americans fifty to seventy) want to continue working in retirement?" this is how they responded:

- Six in ten (59 percent) say staying involved with other people is very important in attracting them to a job in retirement.
- Fifty-seven percent say the job gives them a sense of purpose.
- About half (52 percent) say the job provides additional income.
- And nearly half (48 percent) say the job provides the opportunity to help improve the quality of life in their community.[9]

For women it's even more important, with 70 percent of females age fifty to fifty-nine saying it is very important that a job in retirement gives them a sense of purpose.

A recent article in *Men's Health* magazine titled "Are You Happy? What modern science can teach you about turning that frown upside down," confirms that men have these same heart needs. They studied what makes people happy. Not surprisingly, based on multiple studies, they concluded, "Research has repeatedly shown that increasing your income or even winning the lottery is unlikely to make you much happier, once you get beyond the basic minimum necessary for food and housing."

They quote Harvard researcher Daniel Gilbert in pointing out that "the psychological immune system is also good at explaining away even extraordinarily good events, so that they quickly seem ordinary 'and perhaps even a little dull.' Thus people who pin their hopes on the next big thing often end up on what researchers call 'the hedonic treadmill,' chasing goals that, once attained, don't seem to matter much anymore."

The article goes on to conclude, "We are most likely to achieve happiness, it seems, when it is completely off the agenda. It shows up when we become so totally absorbed in an activity that time hardly seems to exist, and everything flows in the moment."[10]

The MetLife research observes, "This drive contains many of the features of a social movement." So we see some seventy-seven million baby boomers reaching midlife—the wealthiest, best-educated generation, now with an expected life span thirty years longer than one hundred years ago—and many of them are looking for a second-half focus that will engage them in helping others and find purpose for living at the same time.[11]

When historians look back on our time, they may conclude it was either a shining moment in church history, as were those early years during the Roman Empire, or that we squandered the tremendous opportunity God gave us.

The choice is ours. But how do you move from having a deep desire for your second half to be significant to actually living the life you desire? How do you find something that you get "so totally absorbed in . . . that time hardly seems to exist, and everything flows in the moment"?

Your Halftime Journey

Halftime, by its very nature, is a journey. It's not an event, and it's more than just a decision. There are two important tracks to this journey:

1. *The Head Journey*—The Head Journey involves thinking through who you are at the **Core** (your strengths and passions), creating the **Capacity** or margin to begin to give yourself away, and then discovering or designing the ultimate serving **Context** that fits you. This context will include the type of ministry, the role you would play, the work environment, amount of time, and so on.

2. *The Heart Journey*—This is what God wants to do in your soul as he takes you through Halftime to redefine success and pursue significance.

Your Head Journey at Halftime

Moses provides a very clear illustration of the four stages that most people go through as they transition from success to significance.

Stage One: Foundation of Success—Moses spent his first forty years in Egypt getting a great education and working up the ladder of leadership and influence. His focus was on winning in that arena. At the time, I am sure that it seemed like the most important stage of his entire life. By his late thirties he was in a position to influence his entire country if not the world.

FOUNDATION™

OF SUCCESS

In Acts chapter 7, beginning at verse 17, the Bible gives us God's overview of Moses' life.

> As the time drew near for God to fulfill his promise to Abraham, the number of our people in Egypt greatly increased. Then another king, who knew nothing about Joseph, became ruler of Egypt. He dealt treacherously with our people and oppressed our forefathers by forcing them to throw out their newborn babies so that they would die.
>
> At that time Moses was born, and he was no ordinary child. For three months he was cared for in his father's house. When he was placed outside, Pharaoh's daughter took him and brought him up as her own son. Moses was educated in all the wisdom of the Egyptians and was powerful in speech and action. (vv. 17–22)

So Moses was at the top of his game.

While those first forty years were fun and exhilarating, they are not the years of Moses' life that ultimately had the greatest impact. During those years, he learned leadership skills and refined his people skills, which served him well for the rest of his life. He came to understand the systems that drove Egypt, and that understanding served him in his calling later in life. But these early years were merely a platform in Moses' life. They were a foundation of success that God would use to build a second half of eternal significance.

Acts 7 goes on to say, "When [Moses] was forty years old, he wondered how everything was going with his Hebrew kin and went out to look things over. He saw an Egyptian abusing one of them and stepped in" (vv. 23–24 MSG). "Moses thought that his own people would realize that God was using him to rescue them, but they did not" (v. 25).

Like many of us, Moses reached a point in midlife where he questioned his purpose and began to search for something more. Something tugged at his heartstrings. I believe he was experiencing the beginning of Halftime—when we begin to ask, "Is this what I was placed here on earth to do?" We begin to wonder if driving the next quarter's earnings is all there is to life.

This stage represents the end of the first half of our lives, and we begin to ask ourselves:

- Is there more to life than my current situation?
- What on earth would give my life meaning?
- Am I alone in feeling this way?
- How much is enough?
- What is my real purpose on earth?

If you are asking these questions, you need lots of models and stories of what others are doing in their second half. You need a few other people around you who can help you process these tough questions. You need encouragement. You need to know how to work through these issues with your spouse. (We hope this book will help you with all of these!)

In these earlier verses we read that Moses walked out of his office one day and into his community with an eye to really seeing his community through a different lens. He was blown away by the pain, suffering, and need all around him. Something deep inside of him just exploded.

It was a passion God had planted in his heart to make a difference in his world by freeing his people from bondage. But it had been there smoldering under blankets of responsibility, stress, and busyness. Now Moses seemed to have discovered that God-given passion—the reason he was placed here on this earth.

Without good coaching, though, when Moses encountered the needs in his community, he defaulted to his top-down power approach to leadership—and it didn't work. He became frustrated, lost his temper, and killed the Egyptian who was mistreating one of his people. When the news spread, he had to escape to the wilderness.

For Moses, it seemed apparent that God would use his position of power and influence to change the plight of Israel. These verses in Acts tell us that he thought others would see that he was being called to free his people, but they did not. Wasn't his position of influence a wonderful platform to influence the culture? Yes, it was, but God sometimes uses our platform and sometimes chooses to take us out of a prominent position. So, was the first half of Moses' life a waste of time? No. Moses was mistaken, however, to assume that God needed his position of influence to accomplish what he had in mind.

Moses' first half was important preparation for him, but before he could begin to be used by God in his second half, he needed some "Halftime locker-room coaching."

Stage Two: Inward Journey—At age forty, God took Moses out of that prominent role and into a wilderness experience—a time to reflect and retool so that, ultimately, God could use him in world-changing ways in his second half.

The Bible says: "he fled to Midian, where he settled as a foreigner" (v. 29). Moses fled from Egypt into the desert of Midian to take refuge and live for a time in solitude and introspection. God used this time of personal reflection to detox Moses from some of the baggage from his first half so that he could use him to make an eternal impact in his second half. After being a big shot in Egypt, God placed him in a position where he felt like a foreigner, and in the process it appears he learned that his real identity was not found in his position but only in his relationship with God.

He had the chance to reflect on who he was and to begin to listen for God's call on his life. It is quite important for each of us to pause at midlife for an inward journey, and ask ourselves:

- How has God wired me? What are my strengths and abilities?
- What cause or group of people am I most interested in helping?
- In what way can I make a real difference in this world?
- What is my spouse thinking about this next season of life?
- Who can help me make sense out of this time of life?

At this stage you will need a simple assessment of your strengths and passions—time to pray, reflect, and draft a personal mission statement. You need to talk about this with someone who understands your journey and has a good handle on ministry opportunities.

Stage Three: Awakening Challenge—In Acts 7, beginning in verse 30, the Bible says, "After forty years had passed, an angel

AWAKENING™ appeared to Moses in the flames of a burning bush in the desert near Mount Sinai. . . . Then the Lord said to him . . . 'Now come, I will send you back to Egypt'" (vv. 30–34).

CHALLENGE Moses had an encounter with God and responded to God's challenge to live a life of significance. When we receive this renewed vision of who we are and what we were placed here to do, we begin to explore serving opportunities, asking ourselves questions such as:

- What arena should I serve in: the marketplace, my church, my community, or somewhere around the world? Or, perhaps a blend of these?
- How do I start exploring the possibilities?
- How do I prepare my family and myself for this transition?
- How can I make this choice work with my financial situation?
- What is my highest and best contribution?

Moses encountered God and was given his assignment. It was an assignment that fit the abilities and passions God had hardwired into him; and yet it still required faith, risk, and sacrifice.

If you are in this stage of Halftime, you may be wondering how to have an encounter with God so that you know what your real calling is. You wonder what the transition will look like as you reallocate time and energy toward something other than your own success. The real work in this stage is finding and testing out various serving roles and assessing which one(s) fit you best. My co-author Bill Wellons and I want to equip you to start this exploration with your pastor, and yet we don't want you to find yourself limited to serving opportunities within the four walls of your church.

Stage Four: Reaching Potential—Once Moses focused his life's energies in obedience to God's calling, he became an unstoppable force. The last leg of your journey from success to significance is the process of engaging fully in what you are called to do and be in your second half. For many of us, it won't be just one thing God calls us to for our entire second half. Instead we may ask, "Is this right for the next season?" It involves seeking the right balance of serving, mixed in with your career, family, and recreational pursuits.

REACHING™

POTENTIAL

You assess whether you have the "right fit" by asking:

- Does this new blend of family, work, ministry, and recreation work for us?
- Is there evidence that this is God's call on my life?
- Is this sustainable financially?
- Am I growing closer to God and to those I love as I pursue a second half of eternal significance?
- Am I making a difference?
- How does my serving context need to change to be a better fit?

For most people this journey takes months or even several years, and the most important thing is to include others in your thinking: your spouse, a few friends, and your pastor.[12]

So Where Are You? Take a minute and reflect on these four stages. Which stage do you find yourself in right now?

Bill Wellons and I have served, coached, or interacted with thousands of Halftimers across North America. In the process we have learned that, like Moses, they almost always go through these four primary stages. But not everyone goes through them in a linear way, and many of us take a few steps forward and then go back and rethink some parts of an earlier stage—and that's OK.

Knowing what stage of life you are in enables you to focus on what God is trying to do in your life in this season, just as he was doing in each of these four stages of Moses' journey.

Maybe You Are Still in Your First Half. If you are still in the first half of life, you may feel that you need to be "head down" focused on earning a living and raising a family. It seems to me that the Bible affirms this season of life when it says, "It is good for a man [or woman] to bear the yoke while he is young" (Lam. 3:27). Remember that we never read of God putting down Moses for being successful in his first half—it was important preparation. From my perspective, I encourage you to ask yourself a few challenging questions:

- How can I live a well-balanced first half and begin where I am to make an impact for God in the lives of those all around me?
- How can I cooperate with the Lord so that he can create in me the kind of skills, character, and influence that will be needed for the work he may have for me later in life?
- Who do I need around me who will help me to not become overly engrossed with pursuing success at the expense of what really matters? (Do you have a few close friends who cause you to regularly reprioritize your life based on your core values, rather than defaulting to the demands of your career or to social pressure?)

Your Heart Journey at Halftime

We've looked at the four stages of the head journey—thinking through how you will invest your time and talent in your second half. But as I mentioned earlier in the chapter, the heart journey is equally as important as the head journey, but it can easily be over-looked. It will involve a change of heart in at least five areas: creating a new identity outside your career; learning a new way of measuring your performance; discovering the strength of interdependence; finding the confidence to long for intimacy with Christ and others; and seeing the hero in servanthood. (We'll talk more about these five things in chap. 9, after you've launched into the head journey of discovering your second-half calling.)

Before moving to the next chapter, take a few minutes now to read and reflect on the following verses: "What, after all, is Apollos? And what is Paul? Only servants, through whom you came to believe—as the Lord has *assigned to each his task.* . . . The man who plants and the man who waters have one purpose, and *each will be rewarded* according to his own labor" (1 Cor. 3:5–8, emphasis mine).

Now ask yourself four important questions:

1. Based on these verses, what would a significant second half look like for me?

2. At what stage of the Halftime journey do I feel I am? (Foundation of Success, Inward Journey, Awakening Challenge, Reaching Potential)

3. What fears stand between me and launching into a journey toward significance?

4. What questions are most pressing on my heart and mind?

CHAPTER 2

FINDING A BIGGER DREAM

I always had a dream—and then one day at midlife it was gone.

I remember at age twelve dreaming of my first job—I wanted to be a lifeguard that summer, but the rules said you needed to be fourteen. I somehow maneuvered around that and became a lifeguard that summer anyway. Then at age fourteen, I dreamed of buying a piece of land. With a loan from my dad, it became a reality, and I remember walking out onto that first piece of land and dreaming of all the things you could build on it (none of which I did). As the years went by, I dreamed of getting into a prestigious college, of cramming a four-year degree into three years, of building my first house, of paying it off, of reaching a certain level of wealth. By the time I was thirty, those dreams had been realized—and then what?

As I stared at the future without a dream, it dawned on me that all my dreams throughout my first half of life had been within the confines of the career/accomplishment boundaries that were formed early in my life. I saw for the first time that I had not yet found the freedom to dream about something bigger than me, something so all-consuming and significant that it would be worth living the next leg of my life for.

If you are like me, when you watch a movie like *Braveheart,* you're drawn to the character of William Wallace. It is not because he is brave and good looking, although those are desirable characteristics. No, what makes him most compelling is that

he has a cause much bigger than himself that he is living for—
and it's worth dying for.

Finding the Freedom to Dream

Joel's mom had a stroke only a few years after he was born. From
then on she could not walk or talk normally. Life was difficult for his
family, and at age sixteen he left school to become a "tar guy" on a
roof contracting team. But his dream was to buy the company, then
to grow it, and finally to sell it. By age twenty he owned the company, and as it grew, Joel was careful to be not only an honest and
caring boss, but an involved dad and a loving husband. Yet there's
no getting around the fact that he was head down, focused on the
company, traveling all the time. When he sold the business, he had
no idea how to spend the rest of his life. His dreams were all gone,
and he was left staring at a blank canvas with no idea where to turn.

Ralph runs a family business that was founded by his grand-
father more than seventy years ago. He and his wife have three
kids and a busy household. But the industry is changing with new
global competition, and the dreams that drove Ralph in his first
half are waning. When I met them at a couples' conference/retreat
in California, they were exploring what it would look like to discover together a new dream—even one that might mean leaving
their large home on Main Street in small-town America.

A dream is just beginning to emerge in Ralph's heart to be
involved in racial reconciliation among children ages nine to twelve.
He's beginning to explore a wide array of ministries in his area and
around the country that play a part in addressing this issue. The
implications for Ralph are more complex than most of us because
of the generations of family that have been involved in the business, their prominence in town, and the many staff that rely on their
company. As he explores these issues, we process them together,
but what makes Ralph unique among his peers is that he not only
has close friends he processes this with, but he is very open in his
dialogue with his wife. Frankly, I admire Ralph.

Carol has been a family court judge for more than fifteen years, but early this year her husband observed, in a reflective moment, "Honey, I wonder if God has given you these years as a judge to prepare you for some big project or assignment—a big job he wants you to tackle. I suggest you keep your antenna up for what that might be." Carol came to a Halftime event I led a few months ago, and there she discovered that her pastor had a dream that someday the church could make a difference in the families of one district in their city where the average student turnover in elementary school is 120 percent each year. Little did he know that many of the families that come into Carol's court are from that district—she knows them and understands their issues. Now, she is reflecting on what God may have in mind. Was that only a series of coincidences or God's hand at work?

Joel, Ralph, and Carol each have just reached a point in life where it makes sense to move past their first-half dreams and open the door for new ones. Each of them has been head down, focused on their careers for a long time. Each has been successful in different ways, but when they reached Halftime, they needed to find the freedom to dream again.

If they don't, there is the risk they will run too long on their first-half track and end up losing out on the more important things in life. That's exactly what happened to a man I have come to know and respect—we'll call him Gary.

When I first heard Gary share his story, I wanted to cry. Gary is a good guy, a dedicated executive, but he held onto his first-half dreams way too long, and it cost him everything. I shared a brief summary of Gary's story with my wife Linda one evening, and I could tell she was not impressed. She felt he was probably a self-centered, egotistical, money-hungry business guy. But when I showed her a video of him sharing his story from the heart, I could see Linda's attitude change. She turned to me and said, "He's a good guy, but he got lost in the pursuit of those corporate goals."

Gary started his career as a simple sales guy. "They set out so clearly for me that I could go as far up the company as I wanted,

I could achieve as much success as I wanted if I followed the plan. And I did. I did everything by the book, and soon became a manager, moved all around the country—then to headquarters in Greenwich, Connecticut."

So that became his all-consuming dream. Yours was likely different—but perhaps you can relate to Gary. Here's what he told me.

My motivation was entirely focused on myself. I soon found myself enjoying the limos, expense accounts, the big house. I wasn't even in the same state when each of my girls was born. I rationalized it because I had the corporate plane and could get there if my wife really needed me—so I missed the births. I remember saying to my wife on the phone, just before our first child was born, "I will do my best to get there." What a sad answer! I arrived two hours too late. My mom was there covering for me because I couldn't make it a priority.

I reached a plateau in that company, but I was still chasing a dream that drove me higher. It was all too easy to just start returning the calls from the usual string of headhunters. Before long I was faced with the whole next set of rungs in another company so I could keep climbing.

My next company's challenge to me was to lead the sales team from being a regional company to national scope. I tackled that dream with abandon, and what it cost me is breathtaking.

By midlife things were going so good—appreciation in home values, my salary increases, my reputation as a get-it-done guy, and ultimately my success. My wife and girls would go back to Texas for the whole summer, and I worked the entire time. I saw them a few times during the summer, but I felt they were busy and entertained so I was free to just focus on my dream. Little did I know how much they really needed me—much more than just the

money. They needed me there to tuck them in at night—
to hold them, to love them. But I was not there.

I always felt I would make up for it. I said I was going to
change. But I had no other dream to draw me away from
this empty but compelling climb. To make it easier on the
family, I moved them back to Texas permanently—close to
my wife's family and friends. But now, back near her family,
she didn't have to rely on me—much less put up with me.

Ultimately I lost my marriage, lost my girls' respect—
but actually I never had their respect because I never
really respected them. I discovered that I never had a real
relationship with God, or at least one that changed my
life. It all came crashing down all at once—February 6,
2002—and I called my pastor, whom I didn't even know.
"I need your help," I told him. I went out and got on my
knees, confessed so much to God—and my attitude and
my heart were changed by God. Our God is a forgiving,
God and he never gives up on us.

As I was writing this book, I decided to "Google" Gary's
name, together with the national company and brand he helped
build (i.e., I searched the Web). I found that, only a couple of years
after his leaving the company, there is nothing on the Web that
links his name and the brand he sacrificed so much to build. If
instead he had invested in his wife and girls, if he had invested
himself in others around him, today the mark on their lives would
be indelible—a real legacy.

"I am now a work in progress," Gary says, "but I have a changed
heart. Little by little God is showing me what he wants me to do.
I'm finding that so much of his direction is already right there in the
Bible. Jesus came down to earth, and he lived it out for us. Every
time we mess up, we can go to God, and he will help us and give us
another chance."

My heart aches for Gary, but he has agreed to share this story
under a different name because he believes that God can use his

story to help you avoid some of the same mistakes. If, like Gary, you are letting your first-half dreams drive you well into your second half, you might miss out on the impact and adventure that God has in mind for you. If your life looks a lot like Gary's did, I hope that in reading this book you will seriously consider changing course now.

Yes, Gary had a lot of warnings—and perhaps you have too. Yes, it would have been better if Gary had read and listened to what God's Word says about living a life of significance. But he didn't. You can. I am so glad that when Gary finally could see that his plan was getting him nowhere, he went and sat down with his pastor. I am equally glad that his pastor understood him and wanted to partner with him to make his second half very different.

Getting Off the Treadmill

So how do you get off the treadmill, and then, more specifically, how do you find a new dream and reinvent yourself? Take these three steps, and you will find yourself a long way down the road.

1. *Understand the very real risks of staying on the treadmill.* What are some of the things you might lose if you stay focused on what has been driving you in your first half?

Here's a checklist. Circle each of the things that you already know you run the risk of losing:

- your health
- your spouse
- the priceless years when children/grandchildren are young and formative
- your children's respect
- friendships
- time to reflect and enjoy God each day
- your financial health
- recreational time or time for yourself
- the opportunity to make an eternal impact in others' lives
- the role God has for you to change the world
- others _____

2. *Schedule a pause in the near future.* When will you get some time away from the rat race to reflect on how God has created you and what he may have in store for you? If you set aside the time, in a quiet and reflective place, then the following chapters in this book will help provide a simple process for you to work through during that time.

To make this step a priority, fill in the blanks below and then follow through.

I will schedule one full day to stop and reflect on what

I want my second half of life to be about, on _____

_____*, and I will go away to* _____

so that I am not interrupted. I will bring with me only my

Bible, my journal, and _____+_____

_____.

3. *Link up with your pastor.* Begin to pray about talking to your pastor regarding your second half. Ask God to prepare his heart to partner with you to help you find your unique role to make a contribution in the marketplace, your church, community, or around the world. Perhaps consider giving him a copy of this book prior to or during your meeting with him so he can read the reverse side that will help him understand how best to serve you. (We'll give you more detailed ideas later on.)

Now what should Joel, Ralph, Carol, and Gary be doing to discover God's call on their second half of life? None of them, except Joel, is in a position to just quit their job—and chances are that's not what God wants anyway. Instead, they need to begin by discovering who they are at the core—what they are most passionate about—and begin to redirect some of their time, talent, and resources to make a difference in the lives of those around them. That's exactly what they are doing right now—and our next chapter shows how this process works.

CHAPTER 3

THE THRILL OF FINDING YOUR BEST-FIT

A second half of significance is built from the inside out. Each of us is uniquely created and given unique skills, experiences, and passions. Perhaps the greatest thrill in our second half is discovering how those all link together to be used in a unique way to partner with what God is already doing in this world.

Every day I have the privilege of using the skill and experience I learned as a real estate developer, and my abilities in strategic thinking, combined with my passion to help my peers move from success to significance. It's not only fun, but it's also energizing. Frankly, I often see results beyond what I expect. I have a file full of cards and letters from folks saying thanks because their lives have been turned upside down in part through my effort, and they in turn are impacting their world for the Lord. It's not because I am supertalented, but because I have had the opportunity to understand my core strengths and passions, to craft a life mission, and then to ruthlessly live it out. Most of all, when you and I use our unique design to partner with God in something he already is doing, then we can expect to see amazing results.

But it's not accidental—as Ephesians 2:10 says so clearly: "We are God's workmanship, created in Christ Jesus to do good works, which God prepared in advance for us to do."

The Tea Guy

I listened as Kenneth Yeung introduced himself to a small group of Asian American business people by saying, "I'm Kenneth, I'm fifty-seven, and I am a tea guy. I am married, with one lovely daughter, and I am passionate about orphans." I was intrigued. I wanted to know what he meant by "tea guy" and what he did for orphans. He had come to a day-long event I was leading that was designed to help people explore what they would do with their second half.

As he arrived at this beautiful hotel in Vail, Colorado, his secret assumption was that he would be called to sell his company, go to seminary, and become a minister. What he discovered was something radically different, but not at all radically different from whom God made Kenneth to be.

A picture can indeed speak a thousand words, but for Kenneth, it was the words on a poster featuring the photo of a young Chinese girl that spoke to his very soul: "Priority—A hundred years from now it will not matter what my bank account was, the sort of house I lived in, or the kind of car I drove. But the world may be different because I was important in the life of a child."

A native of the Shantou, Guangdong province of China, Kenneth understands more than most the meaning behind that message. Political oppression in China forced his mother to send him to live with relatives in Hong Kong when he was eleven. There he struggled with language and cultural differences, as well as heart-wrenching homesickness. But sensing the hole in his heart and the voids in his life skills, caring neighbors reached out to boost him over the language hurdle and to bridge the gap of his parentless world.

"I learned early on in life that it is so important for someone to give you a helping hand if you don't have help from a family member," says Kenneth.

Several years later, an equally caring teacher led Kenneth to Christ. As he matured in his faith, one thing was certain: he wanted to help others as his way of giving back. He prayerfully contemplated a career in ministry or social work.

"But God had higher plans for my life. He led me to San Francisco, not into social work but into business—and he expanded my influence far beyond what I could have ever imagined."

That business is now a highly successful tea company, but from day one, Kenneth had an unwritten contract with God. "When I started the business, I told my Lord that I wanted to serve him. 'This is your business. I am just your steward to manage it for you.' That unwritten contract guides how I treat my employees— and how I use the funds the business generates."

Kenneth Yeung

The funds his company generates are substantial, but Kenneth says those profits are earmarked for eternal investment, not material gain. He first honored that focus by using profits to help hundreds of American families adopt Chinese children when no agency in America knew how to go about it. In 1993, Kenneth and his wife also adopted a Chinese baby girl, Melissa Joy, who every day of her life puts her fingerprints on the message of the poster that had so captivated her father's heart.

When I asked Kenneth about what he does for orphans, his eyes lit up and he simply said, "Would you like to see my photos? I built an orphanage in China." He reached down and pulled out a dog-eared little photo album and began to show me the most compelling shots of an orphanage for one hundred little children, all of them disabled.

When he got to page 7, it was a photo of him holding a little girl. I was captivated by the smile on his face. So I stopped him: "Who is this little girl, and why are you smiling like that?" He told me her name and said, "I just paid to have her heart transplanted. Without that, she would have been disposable."

Now that took my breath away.

In China, where baby girls are often abandoned, the opportunity to make a difference in the life of a child is great—so great that in 1995 Kenneth began an endeavor that took eight years to bring to fruition.

Considered an embarrassment to their families, the mentally and physically handicapped of China often are thrown into garbage bins. Burdened to make a home for these unwanted children, Kenneth negotiated patiently with the Chinese government. In November 2003, the Prince of Peace Children's Home (POPCH), located in the Wuqing district of Tianjin, opened its doors. Funded by the Prince of Peace Foundation and World Vision International as a joint venture with the Civil Affairs Bureau of Wuqing, the facility can accommodate one hundred mentally and physically handicapped children under six and provides rehabilitation services to other disabled children in the province.

The home sets a miraculous precedent in China: for the first time in history, the government has allowed a foreign organization to build, staff, and manage an orphanage. Today, highly trained staff and caring volunteers lovingly embrace children once viewed as society's trash—and they teach others to do the same.

"I told the Chinese officials that we would not only build and manage the orphanage, but we would also set up a training center to help caretakers from other orphanages in China," Kenneth explains. "What the Chinese government really needs is to see a model that an overseas Christian organization can come in and build this type of thing with love and care. I told the officials that God has loved us, and we want to share our love with the children in China. They accepted that. They even allowed us to engrave a Bible verse on the cornerstone of the building."

At lunch during our time in Vail, Colorado, I asked Kenneth if there was anything else that he is passionate about that he left behind in his first-half pursuit of success. After only a few seconds he looked me straight in the eyes and said, "Well, yes, there is. I am very good at photography. I love photography, but about fifteen years ago I gave it up because my business was growing and my family was busy."

The biggest thrill for me at the end of that day was to sit back and listen as Kenneth shared with his peers a plan for his second half of life. "I came to this day thinking I would sell my business and go to seminary and go into ministry. But," he said, "I'm a tea guy—this is what I do and I am good at it and I make a lot of money doing it. So instead, I am going to hire someone to take some of my responsibilities in my company, and I will go and capture the most compelling photos of disabled orphans in China, print them on the back of the tea packages I sell—to challenge others to help fund an endless supply of orphanages for these children. And I will go and ensure they are run well."

And that is what he is doing today. In fact, he just won a prestigious award by the Chinese government for outstanding charitable organizations—the first non-Chinese citizen to ever receive this award.

As I heard him share this vision, I took a moment personally to simply let his story and the emotions in his eyes sink down deep into my heart and become a vivid picture of what God wants to do in each of our lives. His new life plan includes everything Kenneth is good at and passionate about—it is everything that matters to him merged into one cohesive life calling, unique to him. And it's something God cares deeply about.

Kenneth put it this way: "If I can help change the fate of a needy child, I'd rather do that than have all the world's luxury."

Be sure you capture this one point from the story of Kenneth. It's not the scale of the project that he tackled or the amount of money he is privileged to invest in serving needy children that make his story so compelling. What makes his story profound is the way he was uniquely equipped to play this role.

This should not surprise us. God says clearly that he made each of us uniquely. David captures this best as he reflects: "You [God] created my inmost being; you knit me together in my mother's womb . . . I am fearfully and wonderfully made. . . . All the days ordained for me were written in your book before one of them came to be" (Ps. 139:13–16).

God specifically gave Kenneth an upbringing that helps him care for these children. He gave him business skills that enable him to strategize, network, manage, and partially fund this ministry; and the skill and desire to capture the most compelling photos of disabled orphans that draw others into this ministry.

That is only unique to Kenneth—and there is something unique to you. The question is, will you have the confidence in God to explore, discover, and live out that one thing?

Finding Your Niche

Moving from success to significance and finding your niche involve three primary elements:

1. *Core*—understanding who you are, your strengths, your passions, the role you play best in an organization, and crafting a mission statement that reflects that core.

2. *Capacity*—creating excess capacity (or margin) so that you have time, energy, and perhaps money to begin to give away to serve others.

3. *Context*—develop the context in which you can make your biggest contribution—including the work environment, amount of time, team make-up.

Wende Kotouc was a rising leader within McDonald's (the hamburger store). She is energetic, very smart, and has great people skills. Who wouldn't want her on their team? Most corporate managers with McDonald's stay in an area of specialty, but for some reason she was moved from department to department—giving her experience in information technology, human resources, regional operations, and C.O.R.E. (customer/crew-oriented restaurant experience. It was a demanding and exciting ride, but at some point it simply lost its luster.

Her time during the work week was packed full with her career, but she loved her church (Willow Creek Community Church in suburban Chicago) and wanted to pitch in where there was a need. So on weekends Wende found herself working with infants in the children's ministry. Week after week it became apparent to her that not only did she not particularly like working with small children (other than her own), but she didn't feel that she was really making her best contribution.

One Sunday morning Jim Mellado, executive director of the Willow Creek Association (WCA), walked by her infants' room and spotted her with one darling child on each hip and a forced smile on her face. He asked how her class was going that morning. (It must have been apparent that she was not in her best role.) Jim asked her to consider bringing her first-half skills from McDonald's and joining his team—to not just sell hamburgers but enable churches across the country to better reach their culture with the message of God's love and forgiveness. She took on a COO-type role at WCA, with a staff of more than a hundred and serving twenty-five hundred churches at the time.

It was uncanny how I was prepared for that role through my experience at McDonald's. As I was moved from department to department, I gained experience in the exact four areas that Jim wanted me to provide oversight for. As the Bible says, "God works through different people in different ways" (1 Cor. 12:6 Phillips).

But after fifteen years in corporate America, I sort of felt dirty. I frankly wondered if I was worthy to lead in the spiritual realm. What was so comforting was to see that the skills and passions God enabled me to cultivate in the first half were exactly what was needed in this ministry and, even though none of us is worthy to partner with God in his endeavor, I was welcomed with opened arms.

Wende's core strengths in operational leadership and human and systems development were put into play in a large ministry context only because she was willing to cut back her lifestyle to live on what a ministry could pay someone for this role. Her willingness to live on less enabled her to create the capacity or margin to give herself away—building an organization that has served thousands of churches in more than fifteen countries.

Georgia on His Mind

Your pastor may not be exactly like Jim Mellado—who has an MBA from Harvard and a deep commitment to finding seasoned leaders and letting them lead in the church—but he is the spiritual leader in your community of faith and he can play a very helpful role in your Halftime journey. As you know, the reverse side of this book is designed to help him understand you and to pave the way for you to begin a partnership—a partnership that might look something like this:

Lan Bentsen, the son of the late Senator Lloyd Bentsen, has worked hard and achieved great things in the oil-and-gas business and in new industries in the former Soviet Union. But not so long ago, this think-outside-the-box businessman would have been the

first to tell you something was missing in his life. That something was significance. Even though he didn't know it at the time, Lan had pressed his ear to the wall of his soul. He was listening for God's unique call for the second half of his life. And Lan clearly heard that call at a Success to Significance event that his pastor, Dave Peterson, organized for a few marketplace leaders.

Dave asked me to facilitate a "collaborative day" experience de-

Lan Bentsen

signed to allow him to share his biggest ministry dreams with a few professional people in the church, not only to get their best thinking, but to challenge them to think strategically about how they could best use their unique skills to make an eternal impact. (Details to do an event like this in your church are included in the *Success to Significance Ministry Guide* at www.SuccessToSignificance.com.)

This collaborative day was a time for church pastors and high-capacity marketplace leaders to join together in a strategic thinking session—pooling their most innovative ideas on key opportunities for the church. Lan told me at the start of that day that he was honored that his pastor was specifically asking him to be there and interact, share ideas, and receive encouragement in such a supportive environment.

For each of us it was an invigorating day—and an extremely productive one. In fact, only twenty-two short days after attending the collaborative day event, Lan had put the wheels in motion

on an endeavor that will make a difference in the lives of thousands. Get this: he's taking on the monumental task of reducing infant mortality in the Republic of Georgia.

Like you read in the stories of Kenneth and Wende, Lan has a unique skill set to face this challenge. Several years ago, he led a successful initiative to reduce Houston's infant mortality rate. He's now turning his expertise to an area of the world he is familiar with from his business dealings—an area where infant mortality is ten times higher than in parts of the U.S.

Sameba Cathedral in Tbilisi, Georgia

Lan isn't only dreaming about what he can do. He's making it happen. He has overseen the development of a fully equipped tele-medicine interface with the University of Texas Medical School, and he is actively working to assemble pharmaceutical industry and nongovernmental organizational support. Plans include nego-tiating contracts with the Georgian Health Ministry and obtaining two nurse practitioners, one pediatric doctor, and one ob-gyn. His group will provide the van, driver, maintenance, computer support, and most of the medical supplies. Lan also wants to expand his focus to include childhood immunizations.

"I do not believe any of this would be happening if not for the collaborative day," Lan said. "There I felt, for the first time in my life, the warmth of fellowship and camaraderie that can come from the Spirit of Christ. It was there that I felt comfortable espousing some of my dreams, and it was there that I received encouragement and inspiration. That day was a turning point in my life."

One invigorating day with his pastor exploring opportunities has changed the life of Lan Bentsen and given thousands of chil-dren in the Republic of Georgia what they never would have had— hope for long and healthy lives. He is providing opportunities for others in his church to serve in that country to make a difference, and his pastor could not be more proud of him. His pastor told me that just to see Lan find his niche was worth the effort of the entire collaborative day.

Lan hasn't sold his company or quit his job, but he has found a new dream in partnership with his pastor.

Your Design Statement

Kenneth, Wende, and Lan each took the time to reflect on and even study their strengths and passions, and then to be intentional about how they will allocate their time and resources. The most helpful step is to craft a design statement—often called a personal mission statement. Peter Drucker has told us that a personal mis-sion statement defines for us why we do what we do—our reason for being. For me, having a refined and specific mission statement has been absolutely crucial in trying to choose between the many enticing and high-impact serving opportunities.

Based on what you know about yourself already, take a best shot at filling in the blanks below to create a draft design statement.

What are your core strengths?

_____   _____

What are you most passionate about?

_____   _____

What difference do you most want to make in the world?

_____   _____

Combine the above answers into a simple design statement by filling in the blank equation below:

I will use my strengths in _____ *and*

_____ *to serve* _____

[the cause or people you are most passionate about] in order that

_____ *[the outcome you*

desire to see].

This is something you can refine over time by taking additional assessment tests and through ministry experimentation. Chances are you have done numerous personal assessments already for your career, but if you don't feel like you have a clear enough grasp of your strengths and passions, then here are our suggestions.

Purchase the book *Living Your Strengths* (by Winseman, Clifton, and Liesveld: Gallup Press). It will give you an access code inside the cover to do the online www.strengthsfinder.com test, and the book will help you use your unique strengths in selecting serving roles. Or go online to www.youruniquedesign. org and complete the "Servants By Design" inventory. Then fill in the answers above.

By the same token, you may know already what you are most passionate about—what cause, what group of people, or what difference you want to make in the world. But if you don't, then here are a few suggestions: Your church likely offers a spiritual gifts and passions assessment class. Or attend a Success to Significance Summit near you (listed on www.SuccessToSignificance.com). Even without a formal assessment tool, you can begin to narrow down what most captures your heart. One simple way is to read *USA Today* (or any national newspaper with a global perspective), and rather than read for information, read it and ask yourself, "What stories make me angry, sad, or happy?" When a topic deeply strikes a cord like one of these, then it's worth exploring more.

This goal of understanding your core and creating margin is explored more deeply in my book *From Success to Significance*. With this inward journey completed, it is time to sit down with your pastor. But first we want to help you understand where your pastor is coming from, what makes him tick.

CHAPTER 4

BUILDING A DEEPER RELATIONSHIP WITH YOUR PASTOR

Lan Bentsen is partnering with his pastor and his church to change the world. Sure, he probably could do this ministry alone, but he prefers the sense of community, accountability, and complementary strengths and insights that come with serving alongside his own church.

I know Dave Peterson, Lan's pastor. He's a smart and confident guy, and yet he knows the value of partnering with marketplace leaders, both in terms of the skills, expertise, and network they bring but also for his own personal development. I have seen him interact with very talented men and women as he resists the temptation to put them in a safe place where they can't rock the boat too much (like a committee of some sort), or to buffer himself from their most challenging questions.

I watched one day as a high-powered business owner asked him, "Dave, these opportunities you have presented are great, but what would you say is the core competency of our church?" This was said in a group setting, for goodness sake. All of us would be tempted to put our defenses up. But what makes Dave so good at this is his willingness to not dodge the question or pretend he had a well-analyzed response. Instead, he leaned forward and with a wide smile thanked that business owner for asking the question and asked if he would be willing to help Dave discover the answer to it.

Dave went on to explain to the group why we need to partner like this: "because I often don't even think to ask questions like that." Dave has grown his church to one of the top fifteen Presbyterian churches in the country, and he has every excuse to not be so humble. But he has chosen to. Lan's pastor has intentionally learned how to partner with high-capacity marketplace leaders. In the same way, we want to help you partner with yours.

I have lived both sides of this aisle: as a Halftimer looking for a place to make a difference and as a pastor helping men and women like you find their second-half calling. As a successful real estate developer, I had a hard time finding a place in ministry that fit me. I found the culture gap between the marketplace and ministry very wide. I constantly wrestled with the heart changes God was trying to make in me.

Now over these past thirteen years in ministry, both in parachurch ministries and as a pastor in a large church, I have worked alongside hundreds of Halftimers as they make this midlife transition. I have coached Halftimers from all over the country through their entire journey with regular phone-coaching sessions. I understand at an intimate level how much you need to include your pastor in this journey, how much he needs you, but how very different you are. I have come to respect why this gap exists, and yet there are some simple things you can do to bridge it.

Not surprisingly, as with most things in the kingdom of God, the first steps to building this bridge begin with you. It starts with you making an effort to really understand where your pastor is coming from.

Your Pastor's Perspective

In preparation for writing this chapter, I used three major pastors' conferences as research opportunities. At each conference I was asked to speak to the group about "discovering and deploying seasoned marketplace leaders in ministry." At the end of each session, I asked every participant to answer these questions in writing before leaving:

1. What is the one biggest burning issue you have relative to discovering and deploying marketplace leaders in your church?
2. What most motivates you to partner with Halftimers in your church?
3. What barriers or obstacles do you see churches having as they try to do this?
4. What downsides do you see to doing this in your church?
5. What two key topics should a book written for pastors address regarding this subject?

I want to highlight a few things common to most pastors, based on results of this written survey we did in 2005. The more you understand your pastor, what motivates him, and the things he might be concerned about, the more you will see the need for spending time together and also the value he will bring to your journey. When their collective answers were compiled, here's what we heard loud and clear:

What Motivates Pastors to Partner with Marketplace Leaders?

- The desire to see talented men and women reaching their full kingdom potential.
- To share the burden of leadership with others who are mature Christians and good leaders.
- The potential for God's kingdom and the church.

What Are the Challenges Pastors Face?

- They are not sure how to identify people who are in Halftime, who have a deep desire to make their second half count. (That's why we're encouraging you to be the one who begins this conversation with your pastor!)

- They often find it difficult to come up with serving opportunities that match the skills and interests of such leaders. Sometimes they don't understand the unique sets of skills many Halftimers bring with them from their first-half career. For example, in my church, Norm is a certified nuclear power plant operator. How would his skills apply to ministry? Other times, pastors feel they do not have a vision big enough to challenge the lay leaders. (A learning experience as described in chap. 5 will help you address both of these areas.)

- They want some tips on how to coach Halftimers through this journey. (That's why Bill and I have written two parts to this book. As your pastor reads the pastors' side of this book, it will equip him with all he needs to know to serve you in this journey.)

- They are a little concerned about how to overcome internal cultural impediments to a marketplace leader being free to take on a major project and having the freedom to really lead—impediments like rigid church structure, traditions, and nominating committees, and so forth. (Later in this book we'll help you be better equipped to deal with these potential frustrations.)

The following two quotes illustrate what many pastors are feeling:

"The greatest challenge for me is to learn how to release quality leaders to be as free to dream creatively in ministry as they do in their corporate life."

"I find it hard to develop the God-sized vision that men and women of this caliber could and would give their lives to."

Your pastor likely wakes up every day with the goal to help his church follow God's lead. He probably has a passion to see your church make a difference in the lives of people in your community. But he has a very challenging and often lonely role leading the congregation. The amount of seasoned leadership he needs always outstrips what he can afford to hire, so he needs your help.

Connecting with Your Pastor

Not all pastors are exactly like these survey responders, but with these sensitivities in your mind, your next step is to spend time with him. Meet him for coffee or over lunch. And do it thoughtfully. Here are some specific guidelines for connecting with your pastor:

Step One—Call for an Appointment

- Ask your pastor if he would be willing to meet with you to talk about what God might be calling you to for your second half. Plan on an hour in a quiet setting, such as the office, golf club, coffee shop, or over lunch. Personally, I like early mornings at my favorite coffee shop.
- Know what you want to accomplish in the time allotted. Make notes about your personal story and your desires.
- Pray for wisdom as you seek to build a deeper relationship with him. As you read the rest of this book, reflect on what your pastor's needs and fears might be.

Step Two—Tell Your Story

- Meet your pastor for an hour to share your story: your upbringing, family and spiritual background, education, career highlights, and dreams.
- Tell him where you are now and what you are feeling.
- Ask him to read a copy of this book and talk about it with you.

Step Three—Plan a Follow-up Meeting

- Meet with your pastor again and discuss what you each have learned from reading the book.
- Review with him what you know about your unique design and your personal mission statement.

- Discuss your next steps. We recommend you do a learning experience together.

Step Four—Do a Learning Experience Together

Plan to spend some time with your pastor to build trust and understanding. Perhaps plan to work on a project together, attend a workshop, join him on a mission trip, or work through the *Success to Significance* curriculum. Use that time to get to know each other better and to start to brainstorm how God could use you. (Details in the next chapter.)

Step Five—Find a Best-Fit Serving Role

Based on the self-assessment you have done, the time you spent together, and the projects and ideas you have come up with, begin to brainstorm some ideas for your best-fit in ministry. You'll define the specific *ministry* you are interested in, the *role* you will play, and the *scope of your assignment*.

Your First Meeting

Just to give you an idea of what this meeting with your pastor can look like, let me share an example from what I've experienced. In my pastoral role I've had many of these first meetings. It is somewhat easier for me, having gone through Halftime, to relate to how these people are feeling. I remember my first conversation with my pastor, Jim White. I took him to lunch and shared a little about my family, career, hobbies, and dreams. And then I simply asked him, "What is the single biggest challenge or problem facing the church that I could play a part in fixing?" His response was to pose another question: "What's the one thing you could give your life to?"

Now that was a freeing idea. Not every Halftimer is as bold as I was, and not every pastor is as insightful to ask that kind of probing question. So here's an example of how many of my first meetings usually go.

Mack MacDonald is a big guy with a wide smile. When you see him for the first time across the lobby in the church, you just want to meet him. He's confident, professional, but also warm. Yet he came to me wondering if there was some way he could use his skills to directly reach unchurched people with the message of God's love and forgiveness through Jesus.

I met with Mack several times before he landed in his first ministry role. Our first meeting over coffee was mostly spent learning about his upbringing, education, how he met his wife, their different personalities, some career stuff. He shared his longing for his second half to really count. He talked about how thankful he was for everything in his life, but that there was still something missing. I shared a little of my transition from success to significance and how it is a journey, not an event or a decision. I offered to go on this journey with him. And we have—we are. He's still right in the middle of Halftime.

Mack had done some self-assessment tests with corporate America but needed to do some more—so he took that as a homework assignment. Then we agreed to meet again and explore some ministry opportunities he could experiment with. It was casual and fun. And we both went away encouraged. I was encouraged that he cared so much about God to be willing to, like the Bible says, "offer his body as a living sacrifice." I was encouraged that for Mack, life is not all about him. I think he was encouraged that a pastor in his church not only understood his journey but wanted to share it with him.

At our next meeting we planned an experience together, which was important for both of us. We'll explore that in the next chapter.

CHAPTER 5

SHARING A LEARNING EXPERIENCE

Mack MacDonald and I knew each other from passing conversations in the lobby of the church, but our friendship began at that first meeting in the coffee shop. I really can't remember if he asked me to coffee or the other way around; but after I heard his story, we both needed a higher level of mutual understanding and friendship before we'd be ready to dig into the sensitive issues of Halftime and linking him with a significant ministry assignment.

Building trust and mutual understanding with your pastor requires

- time,
- shared experiences, and
- dialogue, with careful listening.

Mack grew up in a poor urban family and witnessed not only domestic violence but the ravages of alcohol, crime, and poverty all around him. With a bright mind he rose above that and after college began his career at IBM. His heart to serve the poor emerged in his thirties when he felt called to leave IBM to oversee the Charlotte United Way IT department, and eventually he became responsible for overall operations. His wife works outside the home as an executive, and with three children, their house is busy. Still, Mack has a longing to make an even bigger impact in this world for Christ. So how can he live out his desire to serve the Lord with his skills, given his responsibilities at work and home?

Mack and I needed time together to get to know each other, to listen to his musings, for me to share stories of what other success-ful guys are doing around the church and in the community, and to see what fires him up. I think Mack needed to know with certainty that I care about him as a person, not just about using his seasoned leadership skills to tackle a big problem in the church. As a pastor I wanted to know about his relationship with the Lord and his own spiritual maturity. I needed to know if he was servant-hearted and teachable. Was he ready to lead in a spiritual setting?

Most of these issues can be addressed if you and your pastor get together around an active learning experience and begin to build trust, develop greater levels of understanding, and begin to brainstorm how you could match your unique design with ministry opportunities around you.

Three Kinds of Learning Experiences

There are three different types of learning experiences we see happening around the country.

A Hands-on Experience

Work on a short project together. This might be as simple as taking a three-hour "Urban Plunge" to explore several ministries downtown or working on a Habitat for Humanity house for a morning. If your church has a missions program, join your pastor on a foreign mission trip. Generally, this project should take about forty hours of your time, depending on the project's scope, and not last longer than about a month; and it should involve real ministry activity that you and your pastor can do together.

My very first hands-on learning experience was to do a home office relocation study for a foreign mission agency. They knew that their present location was not optimal for their staff, yet they did not know how to determine analytically the best place to move. For me, this provided an exciting opportunity to use my skills in real estate and serve a cause I care a lot about at the same time. As the ministry senior leadership and I worked on this project together, we learned to know and trust one another.

In doing a project like this together, you will also learn more about your passions, you'll expand your understanding of the array of opportunities for service, and you'll experience the culture of the ministry you are considering partnering with. Your pastor will learn to trust and respect you and to see firsthand how God has wired you and how your skills can easily be put to use in ministry. Trust and friendship will begin to form between you and your pastor in ways that won't happen by only chatting in the lobby of the church or in his office.

An Educational Experience

Attend a seminar or workshop together that touches on these topics. Success to Significance Summits are in-depth workshops offered all across the country. Other ministries, such as the Navigators' Second Half Ministries and the Finishers Project, offer outstanding events, many of which are also listed on the www.SuccessToSignificance.com Web site. Each of these events is designed to expand your vision of what a significant second half could be like, to connect you with others who are on the same journey, and give you the encouragement and confidence to take the next steps. Your pastor will gain confirmation from other pastors at this event that Halftimers like you really do represent an unprecedented opportunity for the church and can make a significant contribution to his ministry.

An Interactive Experience

If a Halftime event is not easily available for you to attend, then we recommend that you create an interactive experience by working through the *Success to Significance* small group curriculum

and DVD series together (available through LifeWay or at www
.SuccessToSignificance.com). If you know of a few peers who are
in Halftime as well, consider inviting them to join you in this six-
week experience with your pastor. This curriculum is designed
to enable you to process the heart and faith issues surrounding
Halftime. It brings to you many stories of what others are doing in
their second half and how they have partnered with their pastor.

Recently I led eight people in my church through this six-week
curriculum by conference call. Many successful men and women
in our church travel extensively, so the 800 number conference call
format enabled them to call in from anywhere and be part of a small
group that they would have missed out on otherwise. Through
these calls they were able to get to know me in a much deeper way
and get linked with one another, as well as process the issues that
the curriculum raises. This is a very efficient way to have a meaningful learning experience with your pastor and a few other peers.

Mack's Learning Experience

Mack and I met again at the coffee shop, and this time I had a
specific learning experience I wanted to run by him that we could

Mack MacDonald

do together. We chose to explore a
hands-on, short project to coincide
with the launch of the movie *The
Passion of the Christ.*

It was clear that this movie was
going to sweep across our country and become a pivotal cultural
moment. Our vision for our church
was to take full advantage of the
launch of *The Passion of the Christ*
through a multipronged strategy,
including sending direct mail post-
cards to every household in the area,
booking reserved theater showings

to make it easy for every member of our congregation to invite their unchurched friends to see the movie with them, and then, after the movie, inviting them to a sermon series at the church about the movie. The sermon series would enable them to explore the personal implications of the amazing historical story they witnessed in *The Passion of the Christ*. But, as with every church, our staff was already overcommitted. So who was going to develop this idea beyond a dream? We needed a seasoned volunteer leader to take this vision and first create a strategy and then implement the project effectively—and this was something Mack and I could easily do together. So we partnered for four or five weeks and together celebrated the hundreds of people who came and heard the gospel message as a result of our effort. Most importantly, we learned a lot about each other along the way.

Learning with Your Pastor

Now it's time to set up a second meeting with your pastor to plan an activity to do together that will enable you to learn about each other and from each other. Read through the three ideas for learning experiences and chat about which one you feel will be most beneficial for you both.

Doing something experiential together is unexplainably a part of building a relationship, much less a partnership. When you set aside your formal roles—getting out of your normal marketplace position—it will enable you to begin to understand each other in new dimensions otherwise not possible. And if those experiences are designed to surface issues that are part of the Halftime journey, then you have a winning combination.

Before going any further, there is one point of clarification that I want to make for women in Halftime meeting with a male pastor. While I have had appointments with women in Halftime to discuss their assessment results, to brainstorm ministry ideas, and to help them find their fit in serving the Lord, the more personal aspect of this journey should be processed with a spiritually mature woman.

I recommend that you ask your pastor to identify a female counter-part, possibly your women's ministry leader, to help facilitate this phase of your Halftime journey. If there is not a woman in your church who you feel can play this role, then look for a woman in your community who is known as a spiritual leader. This woman and your pastor can work together later as you craft a leadership role that fits you.

Things to Talk About

Whatever learning experience you select, here are some topics you will want to chat about with your pastor along the way:

- Talk about your inner itch—what's making you want more out of life, as well as the dreams that you may have for the future.
- Begin to brainstorm together—how your skills could be useful in ministry.
- Seek godly counsel—say something like: "You are getting to know me, and I would love to hear what godly counsel you have for me as I approach this next season of life."

To make this very specific, I suggest that you take a spiritual leadership assessment test available online at www.Success ToSignificance.com/leadershipassessment. Print it and share the results with your pastor.

Hear from Mack

I want you to hear firsthand from Mack what this experience did for him.

When approached about *The Passion* movie proj-ect, I was a little overwhelmed by the vision Lloyd put before me. Here was a chance to impact dozens or even hundreds of lives and to be a part of something that had not been done before. On the other hand, there was the dilemma of where I would find the time and energy to do something of this magnitude. I was already heavily

involved with a couple of ministries, as well as other outside interests and volunteering, not to mention work and
family commitments.

But after praying about it, I was made ready, spiritually. Lloyd presented me with some information as well as
ideas for the project. He offered himself as a mentor but
made it clear that the project was all mine. That aspect of
it was exciting and yet unnerving. Although I was a senior
manager in my workplace, I had never done any type of
leadership for the church, nor, at the time, was I looking
to. In fact, I was contemplating cutting back on some of
my activities. But there was something about this project.
The prospect of impacting lives in such a profound way,
through such a unique instrument, struck at my core. And
I couldn't say no to this.

At the beginning, I felt inept, almost like a rookie.
While I had been a Christ-follower for most of my life,
I couldn't come to grips with bringing secular business
processes into the spiritual realm. I felt as if everything in
the church was done through prayer and, with God as the
ex officio "Project Manager," the right things were always
done in the right way. What room was there for workplace
process?

I didn't have time to wallow in indecision, so I did
what I always do, attempted to gain clarity around the
goal, objectives, and resources, which would provide
input into the project plan. Lloyd did his best to assure
me that my business skills were welcomed and actually
part of the reason I was asked to do this project.

In addition to Lloyd's advice, I drew on my previous
volunteer experience. At that level, for the weekly services, everything seemed scripted and accounted for. So
as a volunteer, all I had to do was bring my part and plug
it into the "spiritual machine." As a business person,

though, I knew that there was probably a lot of work that went into planning each activity. At the start, I was probably too conservative in my approach in mustering church resources. Although our church had a nice-sized staff, everyone was busy with their own responsibilities. So, in most cases, if I didn't ask, I didn't receive. It became apparent that I would also need to recruit a team to help.

I found that there was no waitlist of volunteers to pull from, so I had to get announcements done at our weekend services, as well as flyers and information put on the Web site. With the help of some friends, I developed what I needed and recruited a team that coordinated the sale and distribution of tickets for several showings of the movie. We printed and mailed a brochure to more than one hundred thousand households in our community, inviting them to see the movie with us and attend a four-part weekend sermon series to explore what the movie might mean for them personally.

Ultimately, we saw hundreds of people show up. Personally, I was blessed by the experience. But beyond that, what I got out of it was an appreciation for church leadership—what it takes to recruit and motivate volunteers—a deeper appreciation for my knowledge of business processes and project management, and an understanding that just as business gains a multiplier effect from such, the church could too.

I learned that even though it was a lot of work, this seemed to energize rather than drain me. Although Lloyd and the others were very complimentary, I was not sure how good of a job I did. There was no precedent for this, and it was unlike most things in the marketplace; there was no specific target other than to reach as many people as possible. But it connected with a part of me. The staff support and willingness to cooperate, as well as their receptivity to my marketplace skills, was very encouraging. I was almost ready to change careers!

But Lloyd helped me to understand that this was not about leaving what I was good at. Perhaps it was about continuing what I was doing, but leveraging it in service to God. I am still contemplating my ultimate calling regarding my future, but I did connect with something at my core, something that made me long to connect to my reason for being. I loved using my training and experience for such a mission.

You can see in reading these words from Mack's learning experience that this drew us together, helped him begin to really understand how his skills can be leveraged in ministry, and better prepared him as he crafts future leadership roles for his second half.

Like many marketplace leaders, Mack's earlier roles at church were like Limited Partnerships. He put in some money and time, took very little risk, and never had a chance to really lead. This experience was an "Unlimited Partnership" in his scope of leadership, personal risk, and its potential impact.

CHAPTER 6

FINDING YOUR BEST-FIT SERVING ROLE

James Sanders is funny, outgoing, and yet serious about his faith. When we first got to know each other, he was just married, had a fast-growing career in pharmaceutical sales, and was focused on balancing those two important spheres of his life. His wife Susan also has a busy career as a dermatologist. Both of them prayerfully try to be salt and light in the marketplace with those they serve and those they work with.

As James turned forty, however, his thoughts turned toward making an impact for God beyond the marketplace. James came to me to explore what he could do through the church. He was already serving on the Guest Services team and involved in a small group—but what he was looking for was a leadership role that fit his skills, focused on his interests, and would fit around some of the other major obligations and priorities in his life.

But he couldn't just walk away from his career, and his family life was as busy as ever with their children now just reaching preteen years. James is very strong in the area of motivating groups and interpersonal relationships. So we needed to create a ministry role for James that took advantage of those strengths. At the same time, because he travels a lot, he needed a role where he could keep the ministry running even while he was on the road. And he wanted some way that he could redeem the time he spends in hotel rooms and airports. As you can imagine, that required some careful thought and experimentation.

Finding your second-half calling is a process, and often it involves trying several ministry roles before you find a fit. You'll probably experiment with three or four kinds of ministries and a variety of roles, reflecting on what you learn from each one and building on it as you go.

Remember, though, that ultimately your assignment comes from God, and it involves wrestling with God in prayer and reflecting on the Bible's advice—looking for his clear direction. The insights from the combination of intentional ministry experiences, prayer, and reflection, along with your pastor's feedback and insights, is a powerful combination.

The Bible clearly states that God gave you specific skills and interests to be used in a specific role:

- "God has given each of us the ability to do certain things well" (Rom. 12:6 TLB).
- "God has given each of you some special abilities; be sure to use them" (1 Pet. 4:10 TLB).

Three Elements of a Best-fit Role

There are three important aspects to finding a ministry that matches you:

1. Based on your interests, what overall *ministry* should you work in?
2. Based on your skills, what *role* should you play on that team?
3. Based on your life circumstances, what should the *scope of your assignment* be?

Finding, or more likely creating, a serving opportunity that really fits you will take creativity, ingenuity, and always involve risk, both for you and your pastor. You'll need an hour with your pastor and perhaps a few others to brainstorm all the opportunities you can think of that might fit you and align with God's call on your second half of life.

Track with James Sanders to see how this played out for him.

What you know about James so far is he's talented, busy, but longing to use his leadership skills to make a big impact in ministry. But he is very engaged in career and family. As a pastor, it would be simply wrong for me to suggest to James that those things should take second place to the church. At the same time I would not be a good steward of his abilities for the church to be content to leave James in the relatively unchallenging (limited partner) role of greeter/usher. Together we began talking about the roles in his career where he's been outstanding, the things he's energized by. James is great at building relationships, team-building, and motivation. He maximizes the potential of those around him. He is not an administrator or a teacher. We compared those strengths against a list of ministries the church is either already doing or would like to offer. We explored ideas to serve outside the church.

One day as we were hanging out together, he shared a story that helped me see just how talented James is at motivating other men. It seemed to me to be an important piece to the puzzle. He was a motivator even back in high school—you've got to hear his "Cow" story firsthand to know what I mean.

When I was a sophomore in high school, the seniors put a VW bug on top of the school. Their senior prank.

When we showed up that morning, everyone was shocked, but it was so cool. I wasn't sure we could top it. I decided we had to do something special our last week as seniors, so two years of plotting began. I challenged my friends to help me steal a two-ton model cow that was part of the signage for a well-known restaurant in Kansas City and move it miles down the road to the front of our high school. It would be the senior prank of all pranks.

It was a Sunday morning, 4 a.m., when I drove my mom's Cadillac to the restaurant to hook the cow up to the trailer hitch. We had fifteen miles of highway to go. We hung a sign on it—"SMS '81 Seniors"—and reveled in our prank for several days. Then I remember getting that call over the loudspeaker, "Will James Sanders come down to the principal's office?" I was busted! I had been involved in a few other pranks (all very innocent), and the vice principal knew me well. He didn't even ask me if I did it. He proceeded to give me every detail of how we got the cow and put it in front of the school, including the color of my mom's car.

Well, we returned the cow to the restaurant, and I called my mom and told her I was in trouble. Unfortunately, I had to call her from a pay phone. "Mom, I can't talk long. Me and some friends dragged a cow down the highway and put it in front of the school, and I will have to call you back." She called my dad and told him I had stolen a cow from a farmer and dragged it down the road. That must have taken ten years off my poor mom's life.

James Sanders

On graduation night when I received my diploma, the entire seven-hundred-plus graduates said "MOOOO" when I crossed the stage. When I returned home that night after the ceremony, my mother was on the couch crying. "What's wrong, Mom?" She looked at me sympathetically and said, "Why did everyone 'boo' you?" I smiled. "Mom, they didn't 'boo' me, they 'moo'd me." She was so proud!

Now imagine if you could channel that motivational ability for ministry! How do you convince a bunch of peers to do a crazy prank like that? As if you're not going to get caught. He's just gifted at motivating guys. He has since built several successful sales regions for his pharmaceutical company by hiring talented sales people and motivating them to hit their numbers. He mentored many of them to become leaders within the organization.

As we explored ideas, it also became obvious that he cares a lot about helping other men become spiritual leaders in their family, community, and career. I learned this by just hanging around with James and listening to his stories. Again I want you to hear this from him directly.

You've heard guys roast their friends at a party—personally I find it funny. It's never bothered me until several well-intentioned friends of Susan's family attempted to roast me, using stories that they really didn't know well and poking fun in areas that weren't even the most vulnerable areas of my life. All at once I realized that I had no real friends around me—at least friends who know me well enough to really roast me. What a sad deal. I went home that night and couldn't sleep. It was awful to come face to face with what I had become. I love people and have always had friends, but my relentless pursuit of success had crowded out the most important things in my life.

Today my passion for men's ministry comes out of that one sleepless night when I realized I needed to be connected with a few other men myself. I went on to explore a men's small group, reluctantly at first, because I thought it would be stilted and unrealistically spiritual. But instead I found real men with real issues like me. I went on the men's retreat at our church and soon realized that not only did I need this in my life but hundreds of men around me did as well.

Filling in the Blanks

If James used a fill-in-the-blank approach to answering the three big questions I mentioned above—ministry, role, and scope of assignment—it would look something like this:

Based on his interest in _helping men become spiritual leaders_ and _to see unchurched men included in a setting where they can explore Christianity,_ the ministries James might work in are:

    evangelism

    men's ministry

The role James should play in those ministries, in order to utilize his skills as a _communicator, motivator,_ and _team builder,_ are:

    visionary leader

    promoter

    group discussion facilitator

The scope of James' assignment will be determined by how much time he has to give: _ten hours_ (per week) and how far out he can commit to being involved: _twenty-four_ (months).

After learning all this about James, he and I and our senior pastor went and played eighteen holes of golf together. And as we played, we brainstormed several ideas and landed on a place to start. We created a spot where James could provide overall leadership for our men's ministry by building a strong team of volunteer leaders and partnering with paid staff who could provide some of the administrative and event-planning support. This uses James's strengths, undergirds his weaknesses, and fits his life situation. Much of his work he can do while on the road. The life-on-life ministry is largely motivational. The administrative aspects are all off-loaded to others. I want you to hear what James has to say about his role.

Now, I lead the men's ministry, and it's grown and impacted hundreds of men's lives, providing them with godly models, biblical instruction, community, and accountability. Some have come to know the Lord through this effort. Thinking back to that party, I'm now glad for that sleepless night because it awakened in me a passion for men's ministry and forced me to step out and use my leadership skills.

But the payday for me is stories. The story of even just one guy's life can motivate me for months. One high-octane, adrenaline-addicted bond trader came to a men's ministry breakfast. He hadn't been in church for decades, and in this context he began a spiritual journey that has changed his eternal destiny, his marriage, and his family life. When I see him walk by me at church, a thrill rushes through me because of the part I was able to play in him finding a relationship with God.

It's a win-win, where the church has gained a leader who has the vision and passion to run a much-needed ministry to meet the unique needs of men that simply won't get met by attending a weekend service with their family. They need to get connected with other men and process the issues that are unique to them. James has the fun of seeing his skills make a real difference. If you come by the church at 7 a.m. any Sunday morning, you'll find James and his team leading scores of men meeting in small groups at the church. He's found a second-half assignment that fits his skills, interests, and the time he has to give.

Now take a shot at filling in the outline on the next page for yourself.

The Ministry I Might Work In

Based on my *interest* in

_____ and _____
the following ministries might be a good fit for me
(list ideas both inside and outside your church):

_____

_____

_____

The Role I Might Play in That Ministry

To utilize my *skills* in

_____ and _____
the roles that might fit me best are:

_____

_____

_____

The Scope of My Assignment

The scope of my assignment in this ministry will be
determined by *how much time* I have to give and how far out
I can commit to being involved. I have _____ hours
per week/month that I can dedicate to this role for the next
_____ months/years.

After you've given this some thought, set up one last meeting
with your pastor to brainstorm opportunities. You may not find
an existing opportunity within your church, so you may need to
create ideas for new ministries or serving opportunities or reach
out into the community to uncover local needs in existing nonprofit organizations. You may need to explore partnering with a
foreign mission agency to identify global opportunities (explore
www.finishers.org).

The point is that you will someday be held accountable for how you use your time, talent, and resources. And your pastor will be held accountable for his stewardship of you as a resource within the kingdom of God. If you're like me, when I get home to heaven, I don't relish the thought of having to say to God, "Well, I couldn't find something in my church to do because _____ _____ [fill in whatever your excuse], so when I reached Halftime and I had some options, I spent my extra time golfing, doing more business deals, or picking up shells on a beach somewhere."

I know that I don't want to find myself in the same situation as the guy Jesus talked about who was given the talents but buried them because he was afraid. I also don't want to miss out on the great adventure and thrill of seeing God use me in ways that are beyond my wildest dreams. It's not that there is anything wrong with golfing or business deals or picking up shells on a beach. But if you sense God's call to lead a ministry and you take it lightly—and don't aggressively pursue it—that would be a mistake. The Bible put it so simply: "Anyone, then, who knows the good he ought to do and doesn't do it, sins" (James 4:17).

Creative Thinking

This journey from success to significance is not for the faint of heart—and this part of the journey takes creativity, ingenuity, and always involves risk.

So call your pastor and ask him to allocate an hour to help you brainstorm all the opportunities you can think of that might fit you.

This is a unique reverse-read book intentionally to help your pastor create a best-fit leadership role for you. His side of the book provides examples and ideas to prod his thinking, and it's packed full of stories of how Halftimers are serving through other churches. Put all the ideas up on a whiteboard, then begin to compare them with your strengths, interests, and time availability and begin to define possible best-fit roles.

This is a creative process and takes time, brainstorming, and experimentation. Your church may be small and not have a big vision for impacting the lives of hundreds of people in your community. Or your church may have paid staff leading all the major ministries so that it seems that all the bases are covered. Nonetheless, challenge your pastor to come to your next meeting with a list of potential opportunities inside the church, in the community, or even globally that he feels God wants the church to be a part of.

The goal of this meeting is to come away with two or three real roles for you to pray about. Take some time to reflect on them, getting the insights of your spouse and a few close friends. Then pick one and just start. We call this a "low cost probe" because it enables you to "test drive" the ministry without disrupting the other major components of your life.

To gain the most value from this initial low cost probe, you need to work at it long and hard enough to really know how well it fits you and to see if you are effective at it. If you dabble in ministry, you will not see results anymore than I would see results if I dabbled in real estate development—you have to work at it hard.

What if you have a hard time finding a best-fit serving role to test? This is an area where many Halftimers struggle. Here are two suggestions: build a dream team to help you, and tap into some interactive online tools that will help you if you get stuck at this point.

Build a Dream Team

Assemble a small group of strategic thinkers to help you dream about possible ministry opportunities that fit you. This group could include a few peers, your pastor, and several ministry leaders who are willing to dream with you as you refine your best-fit serving role. Give them an overview of your self-assessments and other self-appraisal information to guide their thinking and then cut them loose to dream. Capture all of their ideas on a whiteboard. For a brainstorming session to work well, begin by getting the widest array of ideas out on the table—no ideas are bad ideas. You will be surprised at the level of idea generation that can take place in an hour or two hours. Keep in mind that finding a best-fit match is a process, and don't be concerned if an immediate place of service is not identified.

John Donovan, who leads part of Alpha USA (a ministry that's changing our country), sent us an e-mail about the role of a dream team: "William Wilberforce exemplified this kind of thinking when he formed his 'Chummery' of people who went forth to transform the entire society and its institutions using every social contact they could muster. They never could have had such massive impact if they just got together only for worship and didn't help each other plan how a networking strategy would eventually prevail in the name of Christ." Who's your "chummery"?

Use Online Tools

Bill and I have provided video-based answers to the top hurdles Halftimers and pastors face when they sit down to find a ministry match. Simply go to www.SuccessToSignificance.com/your-questions.

These online resources will help you sort out your calling, even if your pastor is not able to help. Just click on top questions you have as you try to find your best-fit ministry assignment, and Bill and I will give you our best advice by video streaming. We also encourage you to sign up for the Halftime organization's proven, free e-mail-based coaching, *My Halftime Guide*. Lastly, the Halftime organization offers one-on-one coaching through the Halftime Coaching Network. All available at www.SuccessToSignificance .com/coaching.

CHAPTER 7

GETTING THINGS DONE IN THE MINISTRY WORLD

B ob Buford has been a mentor to me for almost a decade. We have spoken at many events together. I have fond memories of him interacting with various Halftimers who were frustrated that their industry and marketplace roles were consuming them. Some feel as if it takes 120 percent of their effort to stay at the top of their game. Bob looks them in the eye and says, "You can change the game, but you can't change the rules of the game."

In other words, there are certain rules to doing business; and if you choose to allocate part of your time to that endeavor, then you will be constrained by the rules of that game. The same is true of ministry. There are certain ways that the ministry world operates that are different from the marketplace. Jim Collins, author of the best-selling business book *Good to Great,* has spent some time in recent years exploring what "good to great" looks like in the social sector. His advice about how to get things done in ministry settings is: Do not assume your business success will cause you to be successful in a nonprofit. The metrics are different. "In business, money is both an input (a resource for achieving greatness) and an output (a measure of greatness). In the social sectors, money is only an input, but not a measure of greatness."[13]

There are ways of getting things done in ministry that are very different from getting things done in the marketplace. There are three primary categories of these differences:

1. Supernatural
2. Organizational
3. Cultural

Supernatural Differences

Let's get the openly spiritual differences on the table first—the supernatural. You may experience spiritual or ideological opposition to your work. You will wonder how to sense God's leading in the direction of your ministry, or how to know for sure where God is at work so you can join him. These ideas sound sort of nebulous compared to hiring an ad agency, for example, to do market research. The prospect of really understanding them and working with them seems intimidating for many of us business people.

It's true that nothing really happens in the spiritual realm without God's Spirit making it happen. It's also true that, strange as it may seem, God's strength is often revealed in areas of our weakness. You may not have encountered these supernatural issues in your business or professional work. So how do you prepare to do ministry in this wholly new space?

Chances are you have been following God for some time now. You have learned to seek God's direction as you and your family have made important decisions about jobs, moves, health, financial issues, and so forth. The good news is that seeking God's mind and direction on ministry leadership issues is no different.

The biggest risk actually may be the perception many Halftimers develop that, since their business skills enable them to lead well, they operate under the illusion that they can "handle it" with their own talent. But that is not true. For our ministry effort to be at all effective, we need the Lord to provide the wisdom and to work through his Spirit in people's lives. So let's train our hearts to understand that what we can seemingly handle on our own strength can be completely unfruitful ministry if we are not listening to the promptings of God.

Simply apply the same disciplines that you do when you and your family encounter other issues in life that are obviously beyond your control:

- Go to your Bible for wisdom
- Pray
- Reflect
- Listen

One of my first ministry experiences was to lead a project to take about one hundred Christian farmers to Albania in 1993, just after the fall of communism. It was a partnership between the Albanian Ministry of Education and SEND International (a mission agency—www.send.org), designed to aid farmers in their transition from centrally planned farming to market-driven farming. Albania was one of the most staunchly atheistic countries in the world, so our goal was also to serve these farmers by sharing with them the message of the love and forgiveness of God through Jesus Christ.

When I was asked to lead this effort, I wondered if my skills as a real estate developer really would translate into that arena. After only a few weeks, I could see that this project used my project management skills, my marketing skills, even my sales ability as I tried to influence people on both sides of the ocean. My experience in developing budgets and managing expenses was also important. The creative problem-solving, which every successful real estate developer learns, was needed in missions as well. I soon began to believe that I really was prepared by my first-half career to excel in leading a ministry that was taking the gospel to communities that had not heard it for more than seventy years. I was both encouraged and naive.

I was not really prepared for the spiritual opposition to the good work we were trying to do. For example, every team of Christian farmers that arrived needed a few nights in the capital city of Tirana for orientation before traveling to their designated village. I had arranged hotel rooms for every team and every participant months in advance, confirmed in writing. Yet every week as a new team arrived, I would go to the manager of the Hotel Tirana to confirm that the rooms would be available when I got back from the airport, only to have him give me some reason why they had to give our rooms away to the UN or some other more prestigious group. At that time there really were no other hotel options. We'd eventually get the rooms (or most of the rooms) we needed.

Finally, in frustration one week, I said to my ministry partner Eric Palmquist (who had been a missionary in lesser-developed countries for years), "I am so frustrated. I am just not negotiating well with these people. For some reason I can't seem to find a win-win approach where it is worth their while to make sure we get the rooms we need." Eric looked at me and in a teachable moment explained what he had known all along: "Lloyd, this has nothing to do with negotiating; this might be something spiritual. This might be something you and I can only win through prayer. Forget about negotiating harder, and let's pray about it." There will be times in your new ministry work when working harder is not the solution, and being smarter is not the answer—because we are working in a spiritual arena.

The Bible is also clear about the spiritual authority that God gives to those who lead in the church. Your role may be under the spiritual authority of your pastor, and you wonder what that means practically. Jay Bennett is a successful lawyer in Minneapolis. He reached midlife and began to explore how he could make a difference for God in his city. He's learned something about this idea of spiritual authority and partnering with your pastor that I think you'll find interesting. Over the past ten years he's been gradually allocating more and more time to a ministry he has started called Kingdom Oil (www.kingdomoil.org), equipping and networking people who want to invest in ministries in their community.

Recently, a complex health problem took Jay's voice away, leaving him to go through months of mostly listening. From my observation, during this time Jay learned to listen more deeply than most of us do. When you have a hard time speaking, in addition to listening more, it forces you to boil down what you say to just the most important things.

Today Jay's voice has returned, but the habit of listening remains. Here's what Jay has learned along the way.

Pastors need to find the personal and institutional freedom to equip and release marketplace leaders, but not just releasing them to church-budgeted activity. That would be like an aircraft carrier where most of their jets are safely stored below deck, and others are assigned missions to fly around the carrier. Instead, the key is to release them fully into enemy territory and then call them back for patching up and refueling.

We as successful marketplace leaders, in turn, need to submit to the spiritual authority of our pastor and progressively pursue deeper spiritual maturity, moving from a place of worldly success to significance but ultimately surrender. This cannot be done by getting a flash of inspiration and then running out in our own strength to fix a problem.

It reminds me of the rifles used during the Revolutionary War. If soldiers panicked and did not fully cock their rifles, when they shot, it would fire off to one side. It would "go off half cocked." If a Halftimer isn't following God and doesn't operate under the spiritual leadership of the pastor, they run the risk of going off half cocked—and missing the target. When both the pastor and the Halftimer are consulting with God and submitting to the authority of one another that God has designed into each, then their unity at the cross allows them to partner and serve one another.

This is modeled in Acts chapter 6, where a cross-cultural issue arose in their community. The Hellenistic

Greek widows did not speak Aramaic. They were a different people group, and inequities had begun to impede the spread of the Christian message. But because both Peter (the pastor) and Stephen (the marketplace leader) were consulting with God, there was freedom for those in spiritual authority to appoint those gifted to serve in culturally relevant ways.

Jay Bennett (left) and His Ministry Partner

We recently saw this same thing happen here in Minneapolis. Our ministry, which I named Kingdom Oil, opened a donor-advised fund to deal with the integration of African American evacuees from Hurricane Katrina, and we put $200,000 in the hands of black pastors with a couple of business types acting as advisors. White suburban churches gave. The Minnesota Twins gave. It was a kingdom thing. The effect was an experience similar to Acts 6—the power of God surged through this reconciling model of loving God and loving our neighbors as well.

This spiritual element involves understanding that there will be spiritual opposition, prayer, listening to the promptings of God, and being willing to work under the leadership of your pastor.

Organizational Differences

Getting your head and heart around the spiritual differences between the marketplace and ministry will go a long way toward helping you be effective. Another area that is important to understand is how differently ministry is organized and how it operates. To avoid frustration around these organizational differences, make sure you have the details clear—in writing. Some of the most important things to be clear on as you start are practical and systems-oriented, such as defining the scope of your work, having a job description, budgeting, and accountability.

Here's a punch list:

- What are the goals or expected outcomes of your ministry in six months/one year?
- Who will you report to?
- How will the appropriate staff know about your role?
- Where will your office or work space be?
- How much of your time will it take to be effective in this role?
- How does the church run, from an organizational and financial perspective?
- How does budgeting and expense management work?
- How will you promote your ministry? (Web, bulletin, platform, e-mail, video, etc.)
- What administrative support will you need, and how do you access that in a way that blends with other demands on the staff?
- How will you link with the church database?
- Who is best positioned to help you find the volunteers you will need?
- Who is your "go to" person if you get stuck or frustrated?
- Will you be paid something or do this as a volunteer?
- How do you access office supplies, phone, computer use, e-mail?

Before you begin your assignment, talk with your pastor and get answers to these questions so that you will be clear about your position. If you will be working with someone else on the pastoral staff, confirm these details with them so that there will be less chance of misunderstanding. Discuss if your project overlaps with other leaders' work, or if there are existing ways of doing things that you may not be aware of. Then be creative about how you can accomplish what you need to with the minimum amount of disruption in areas of sensitivity. Ask yourself the question, "How can I make this whole thing better without crossing a line needlessly and creating conflict?"

Cultural Differences

The third area where the marketplace and ministry are very different is the culture. Every organization has a unique culture, and yet there are common themes that we hear over and over as Halftimers plug into ministry. This issue is a little more sensitive to talk about. As a pastor, I have seen that it is not uncommon for a Halftimer to find his place to lead, and before long they share with me how different the culture seems to them:

"The pace of decision-making is sooooo slow, it drives me crazy."

"Around every corner there is some closely held tradition that impedes our innovation."

"It seems like we are just speaking a different language."

"I find it so hard to really push the team for results or even know when our work is being effective."

Behind these remarks is a bedrock of culture that can derail even the most persistent Halftimer. Here are some examples of the most prevalent ones.

1. Tradition

Traditions and an unwillingness to change sometimes suffocate marketplace leaders in ministry. My brother Jim has led the real estate consulting arm of several major international accounting and consulting companies, teaches as an adjunct professor at the Penn State school of architecture, and has owned his own business—you name it, in corporate America he has experienced it. He's a thinker. That's how he solves complex problems for some of the leading companies in our world. We're together for holidays at least four and sometimes five times a year. When our families are playing on the beach or watching a movie, we often talk about what we both love—thinking through complex issues in our individual areas of expertise.

For more than a decade he has listened to my stories and musings about the cultural gap between the marketplace and ministry. One day, he offered an observation that has helped untangle some of the issues you will experience as you try to bridge between these two worlds. "The more money that's at stake in a business transaction or an enterprise," Jim observes, "the less individuals will become polarized over issues like traditions, mannerisms, language differences, and so on. When you take this material reward component out of the equation, each player tends to focus on ideology, personal turf, and traditions."

I think Jim is onto something. Some leading Christian thinkers have all but given up on the church being able to really partner with marketplace leaders because of this impediment. I believe, however, that once you understand why traditions are held so tightly in most churches, then you can begin to redirect this controlling, inward orientation outward. You need to lift people's sight above the minutia to catch a vision for the big picture by sharing a compelling vision of the impact your ministry could have. In essence, you are giving them something big enough to work toward together that the small things of turf and tradition fall by the wayside.

I recently spoke to a group of one thousand seniors who are interested in finishing their lives well—using their latter years to make an impact for God in their community. Over the three days, I shared with them story after story of seniors I have met around the country who have moved beyond entertaining themselves, beyond just the next bus trip to see the fall leaves, to using their wisdom and experience to serve others. I told a story of Lloyd Howe in Indianapolis, a seventy-year-old entrepreneur who has started more than twenty companies in his lifetime but now is having the time of his life placing older adults as paid teachers' assistants in the worst elementary schools in the city. I described to them the look in his eyes when he told me that today three of these schools are now blue-ribbon schools.

As I went to leave this gathering, a seventy-five-year-old lady came up to me with tears running down her cheeks and said, "I need to just tell you—my husband died last month after I cared for him through five years of Parkinson's disease. You have so inspired me to use the rest of my life to serve the Lord—I am going to give my life away—and I can't wait to see what God does with me."

Do you think that lady is going to whine to her pastor about the style of music they use for the new outreach service or the color of the carpet? Because we cast such a compelling vision for her of what her life could be about, she is way past that pettiness.

As you encounter turf issues, bureaucratic hurdles, and traditions, make an effort to point people beyond those issues to what could be.

2. Measuring Results

In the church, we really give a standing ovation when an outreach event goes well, or when lots of people show up for weekend services, when we sense that our constituents are mostly happy with the programs being offered. All of these are great, but are they results? These are indicators that we may be producing the results we desire, but the church was not placed here on earth to fill up seats and run programs. Do we know what real results would look like? We long to see people's lives and eternities really change, but it is hard to measure that.

Chances are that in your marketplace role you have created a culture of measuring bottom-line results. You may have found effective ways to measure customer satisfaction as an indicator of how well you are delivering value to the customer because you know there is a direct link between that number and your future sales and profits. Nonetheless, there is a clear indicator of what results really are—profits.

So you'll have to reorient your metric of success when you begin to lead in a ministry setting, and that likely won't come naturally.

Most ministries gauge their performance by inputs, not outputs. This is in part because it is hard to measure outputs in a spiritual enterprise. For example, the mission of the Halftime organization is "To inspire and equip marketplace leaders to embrace God's calling and move from success to significance." The temptation is to measure our results only by how many people read our books or visit www.SuccessToSignificance.com or sign up for online tools or attend our events or the number of churches that launch Halftime ministries.

These are indicators, but they are all inputs. What we really need to measure is how many successful people discover God's call on their second half and actually reallocate their time and talent accordingly. But that's very hard to measure, so we tend to settle for measuring inputs, and then we comfortably rely on the verse that says, "I planted the seed, Apollos watered it, but God made it grow" (1 Cor. 3:6). In other words, we just leave the real results up to God and don't bother to measure them.

There are good points on both sides of this issue. You and I run the risk of only focusing on performance as quantifiable outcomes—when in God's economy there are times he calls us to be faithful and follow him and the results will not be clear this side of heaven. We, as marketplace leaders, need to bring to the team a much-needed discipline of measuring the real outcomes and prayerfully considering deploying resources toward the higher yield of fruit we see.

3. The Value of Graciousness

Nearly every ministry culture I've experienced or worked within has the leading value of graciousness. But in my first ministry leadership role I remember wondering, *How on earth do you drive performance in a space where everyone is supposed to be gracious with each other?* Graciousness in a ministry culture can be manipulated in two dysfunctional ways: (1) a certain sweet, almost sappy way of interacting that masks the real and normal range of human emotions, or (2) lowering expectations or standards of excellence. Neither of these really honors God.

On the other hand, many marketplace leaders (myself included) have learned aggressive, take-it-or-leave-it mannerisms that don't work well in an environment where most of the team are volunteers.

Suppose you're leading a ministry in your church and you need the media crew to create a promotional video; but when you ask them, you find they are already busy on an assignment for the senior pastor's upcoming sermon. Or perhaps you need regular use of facilities that often are overbooked. How do you negotiate for what you need without being either too harsh or not assertive enough?

Perhaps the most practical verse to help you learn to bridge this culture gap issue is "speaking the truth in love." Say what you see or need without dropping the standard, but do it in a way that reflects God's love for the individuals you are ministering to or with. In so doing you will help the entire team to recalibrate what graciousness really looks like in a healthy setting.

4. Your Language

As in any culture, what you say has meaning in a certain context. At times, the terms and mannerisms you normally use in the marketplace will communicate something different from what you intend to your ministry partners and may cause them to question your motives. Be aware of times when you use phrases, as I have often done, that may not be understood in ministry. And your ministry partners will use church language that you may not understand.

For example, as you begin to build a strategy for your ministry, chances are you will find yourself talking about marketing the ministry or defining who the customer is. As you do, your ministry partners may be thinking, *We don't have customers, and we aren't trying to sell people on Jesus.* It's challenging for a person who has been in ministry all of his or her life not to feel as if you are trying to turn ministry into business. They may attribute to you a sort of cold, merchandising heart, when in fact these words simply reflect how you think.

Let me give you some simple strategies to alleviate this pitfall. Get this issue out on the table. Let your ministry partners know up front that when you use your native business language you are not trying to turn ministry into business—that this is just your normal terminology. Make a habit of going back to your team regularly to confirm their understanding, and be willing to adopt some new language over time.

5. The Degree of Urgency

Seasoned ministry leaders know that, as Henry Nouwen said, "God is never in a rush." His timing is perfect, and the last thing we want to do is to get out ahead of God. They may have a healthy balance in their personal lives that enables them to confidently leave their ministry work at the end of the day and refocus on family and recreation, knowing that God commands a Sabbath.

However, they may never have experienced the kinds of intense pressure that marketplace teams put on themselves to achieve superior results. They can learn from you in this area, and you can gently cause them to do a gut check about how urgent their ministry really is to them. Do this in a way that still allows you to be a learner of all that God has taught them about his timing and pace.

If you lead in corporate America, the next quarter's earnings are reported every ninety days, whether you like it or not. If you are a principal, your school will be assessed based on end-of-grade tests that your kids take—and those results will likely be benchmarked and published for all to see—whether your team was ready or not. That gives a certain urgency to your leadership, right?

But when you are leading a ministry, there is often no regular day of reckoning. As such, the culture of graciousness and the soft assessment of performance makes it all too easy to drift. Not always, and not in every ministry, but this is true in many, if not most. So you will find it frustrating that the sense of urgency is higher in your marketplace role than in ministry, where you feel urgency should be higher. After all, eternity is on the line.

Just know that there's value on both sides of this issue. Bring your sense of urgency, but with it bring a broader understanding of how God works in ministry.

6. Leadership Styles

One area where the culture gap is narrowing is in the area of leadership styles—in particular around the idea of servant leadership and emotional intelligence. Top down, heavy-handed leadership has been having diminishing returns in the marketplace as our workforce has become more independent and portable.

As you begin to lead in ministry settings, you will be forced to learn to lead even more as a servant leader—and that, in turn, will help you lead more effectively in the marketplace. I teach a one-year program in our church for marketplace leaders who want to learn to lead like Jesus at home, in their community, and at work. The benefits all around are astounding. Part of this curriculum involves a monthly conference call. They're focused on application through peer interaction. As I hang up at the end of these calls, I am almost always amazed at how relevant the model and teaching of Jesus is for these men and women.

For example, two primary impediments of effective leadership are fear and pride. These two attributes are seldom discussed openly in our marketplace settings. You could go on for decades withholding information so that you retain control, not delegating effectively, and taking credit for innovation your team developed because of fear and pride—and no one would help you label those and root them out. So you can use your ministry experience to begin to ask yourself, "How are fear and pride hindering my ability to really lead?" How did Jesus lead differently?[14]

The whole idea behind moving from success to significance is to live a life that is great. There was a time when Jesus' disciples were arguing about who was going to be the greatest in their ministry roles. Each of these men had been called to take time away from their marketplace roles to lead in a ministry setting, and they wanted their lives to be really significant. So here's what Jesus said: "You know that those who are regarded as rulers of the Gentiles lord it over them, and their high officials exercise authority over them. Not so with you. Instead, whoever wants to become great among you must be your servant, and whoever wants to be first must be your slave—just as the Son of Man did not come to be served, but to serve, and to give his life as a ransom for many" (Matt. 20:25–28).

Notice that he never got on their case for wanting to be great—or to live lives that really amounted to a lot. He didn't try to untangle which elements of their motivation were pure and which elements were not. Instead, he completely redefined what it means to be great.

The implications are that leading in a ministry needs to be grounded in the bottom-up, serving style of leadership we see modeled by Jesus. As we learn this, we can apply it in every setting—the marketplace, our community, and of course our family—by serving others as we lead them. And as we do, we will see results. As Jesus said, "Command those who are rich in this present world . . . to do good, to be rich in good deeds . . . . In this way they will lay up treasure for themselves as a firm foundation for the coming age, so that they may take hold of the life that is truly life" (1 Tim. 6:17–19).

And that's a good thing, and worth celebrating.

CHAPTER 8

CELEBRATING YOUR RESULTS

Peter Drucker drummed into our heads, through his more than sixty years as the foremost management guru, that we value what we measure. And we need to measure results, not activity. This discipline is somewhat more complex in the ministry realm, but it is an important part of your ministry and of what you can bring to this arena. In order to celebrate results, you need to measure them. Also, as you stop and assess the results, it provides an important time for you to adjust how and where you serve. This midcourse correction is normal and important as you seek to find a new equilibrium in your second half.

Celebrating the results of your ministry is also an important discipline. Celebrating might sound more like a party than discipline, but it requires discipline to pause periodically and just celebrate together. As one season or project comes to an end, it's all too easy to get caught up in the next round of ministry and forget to stop and be thankful for what God has let you be part of. As you discipline yourself to stop and celebrate together as a church, you will cast a vision for other Halftimers to pursue significance.

I walked through the front door of a beautiful home in Newport Beach, looking forward to a relaxed dinner and the chance to hang out with about ten men and women who were hosting a Success to Significance event I would lead the next day. Cliff Ratkovich was listening to some of his peers share career and ministry stories. I introduced myself to Cliff and found out he was also a real estate developer. We swapped war stories, and Cliff shared with me that, as a fifty-one-year-old real estate developer and one of the largest home builders in California, he was constantly under the gun. He had no margin in life, yet he felt called to launch a unique ministry in his community through his church. He briefly described what he had in mind and wondered aloud if it was truly God's call on his life.

As someone who loves sailing, I know that you cannot steer a sailboat that is standing still. You have to get it moving to be able to steer it. So I said to him, "Cliff, God can't steer your boat if it's tied to the dock. I suggest that you cut the lines, lift the sails, and see where God takes you." So he did.

A year later when I was back in Newport Beach, Cliff told me that after discussions with his wife, his pastor, and his company, he had left his job and set out to build a ministry called HopeBuilders alongside his church. "Lloyd, when you were here last, you said, 'To steer a sailboat, you've got to put it into motion. And if you wait for everything to be completely worked out—lined up perfectly and all your financial resources in place—you'll never pull the trigger.'

"Well, I don't have it all figured out, and I may not have all my financial ducks in a row, but my slant is, if I don't do it now, when will I do it? And what I've learned thus far is this: If you want to take the ride of your life, and feel more connected to God than you've ever felt, and experience joy and satisfaction that you can't get in the marketplace, then you've got to take the plunge!"

HopeBuilders "builds hope" by improving the physical living conditions of needy families and individuals. A short nine months later, Cliff and 150 volunteers were cheering (and, truth be known, crying) as the eleven members of the Arancivia family exited a van and wept at the sight of their newly remodeled home.

Prior to its extreme makeover, the 1,600-square-foot house, where generations of Arancivias had lived, sported a weary single-sink bathroom, a leaky roof, crumbling walls, a kitchen with "Fire

Hazard" written all over it, and numerous other repair needs. To the amazement of all, HopeBuilders volunteers, funded by private donations and corporate sponsors, had completed $150,000 worth of structural remodeling and interior decorating in only ten short days.

Although HopeBuilders was already on the ground building hope prior to the launch of the hit TV series *Extreme Makeover— Home Edition,* the ministry has benefited from the nation's passion for the show. Sponsors and volunteers quickly grasp the concept and can visualize themselves lending a hand, even if it's simply a hand with a broom in it.

In addition to the first major makeover, HopeBuilders volunteers have completed mini-makeovers for disadvantaged college students, a sixty-resident homeless women's shelter, and the Orange County Chapter of Teen Challenge, which houses dozens of male residents who are working hard to get off drugs and alcohol—and the list continues to grow. In addition, the ministry recently introduced a prototype house or "shack" in South African squatter camps, where living conditions are deplorable. Once again, Cliff's history of innovation is making a difference in their lives.

"We feel God's pull locally and internationally as well," Cliff said. "We want to use our skill-sets to help fix a broken world."

Aching backs, bloody hands, dirty fingernails, soaring hearts—these are the tools of the trade that forever change lives. "Truth be known," said Cliff, "our hearts are changed far more than those whom we set out to help. The families we select to serve have real needs, and we're doing it as a way to show God's love and to improve the quality of their broken lives. But they are really a vehicle to create an opportunity for HopeBuilders' more than five hundred volunteers to engage and to experience God's transforming presence."

"This is a reward you don't get from your nine-to-five job," one volunteer said with a sunshine grin on his face. "I'm absolutely addicted to it."

OK, sounds heartwarming, but what are the real results and how do Cliff and his team celebrate?

You can see imbedded within this story several measurements: the number of families served, the dollar value of the contributions, the number of volunteers. Harder to measure are the life changes that occur in both the families served and the lives of the volunteers. But the celebration takes this impact to a whole new level.

Celebrate HopeBuilders

Cliff's church captured the story on video and shared it with the whole congregation. As an entire church, they had a chance to celebrate. You really have to see this story personally with your own eyes and celebrate with Cliff. Take a minute now to go online and watch a short clip of the very first home Cliff's ministry did (www.SuccessToSignificcance.com/hopebuilders). And as you do, think about what this celebration will be like in your own life when you cut whatever lines are holding your boat to the dock, lift your sails, and see where God takes you.

Bruce Nelson is one of Cliff's pastor at Mariners Church. I asked Bruce to share how he feels about this journey he and Cliff have gone on together. Cliff did not see this note from his pastor before this book was sent to the publisher—and I know it will not only warm his heart but encourage thousands of other Halftimers to take a risk and begin this journey with their pastor.

Dear Cliff,

It's been amazing to watch the journey you and Rose have been on over the past year, and I just wanted to share with you how thrilled I am. The transformation in your life and the impact you have made have been really remarkable. How does God get hold of a successful real estate developer to the point where he will leave his role as president and invest his life blessing the poor and needy? Your life has been a powerful example of seeking and following God's call. You heard God's voice and responded with your life. As a leader, you passionately shared God's vision, recruited other capable leaders, created a strategy, and coordinated a team of more than five hundred volunteers—a truly amazing accomplishment! But what touches my heart the most is seeing your humility as you have learned to rely upon God. When it looked like plan A was impossible, you learned to release your grip, knowing that this is God's project after all. You have drawn closer to God, and I am so honored to have been a part of this journey with you. Thank you for being such a blessing to me and to so many others.

Love, Bruce
Men's Ministry Pastor
Mariners Church (Newport Beach, California)

This letter is part of the celebration—one-on-one, the pastor and marketplace leader pausing to high-five each other along the way. But if you're like me, the letter challenges you to re-up for God's next assignment in your life.

When your ministry project is complete or when your work reaches a natural break point, call a time out and assess the results, debrief with your pastor, and then celebrate with a wider community within your church. In a very real sense this is an act of worship. In Acts 19, this is what Paul did when he came to the end of a hard ministry assignment: "The first thing next morning ... [a]ll the church leaders were there. After a time of greeting and small talk, Paul told the story, detail by detail, of what God had done among the Gentiles through his ministry. They listened with delight and gave God the glory" (Acts 21:18–20 MSG).

Let's take a closer look at what Paul was doing. The church leaders were there because they were interested. It was friendly and relational, not corporate. Paul told stories because they engage the heart, but he also provided details because we not only see God's hand in the details but we learn from them for the future.

How to Celebrate

When you meet to debrief your ministry experience with your pastor and the church leaders, we encourage you to address the following important issues:

- Thank your pastor for helping you find this second-half assignment.
- Restate the vision, mission, and goals of your ministry.
- Present the results in a simple way.
- Share one compelling story of a person who was impacted by your ministry in the way you have envisioned.
- Ask them for their observations and assessment in terms of (1) your fit for this role, (2) the overall results of the ministry, (3) ideas they have to improve it, and (4) what should the plan be for going forward?

Back to where we left off in Acts 21. Remember how it says as they listened they were encouraged, then together this community of faith worshipped God as a result of one person's ministry? This is what you, your pastor, and the whole church can experience together. Ask your pastor specifically how he feels you can best celebrate *"what God has done through this ministry, so that others can listen with delight and give God the glory."* You might not produce a professional video like Cliff's church did. It might be a simple article in your newsletter, a feature story on the church Web site, or a short testimonial on Sunday morning with time for the church to worship.

Lastly, as you celebrate, make it clear how others can begin the journey that you and your pastor just experienced together—others who are perhaps experiencing Halftime but have never dreamed of what it could look like for them. Specifically say to the congregation, "If you have a longing in your heart to move beyond just pursuing success to significance, please come chat with me. I would love to share more of my journey with you, as well as some specific next steps you can take."

Then give them your copy of this book—and you will have just created a Halftime movement in your church!

CHAPTER 9

THE HEART JOURNEY AT HALFTIME

I introduced the idea of the Heart Journey at Halftime in chapter 2, but now I'd like to further explore what that really means. Let's recap. You've found your ministry, and you have reallocated some of your time and talent to make an impact for the Lord in addition to your normal marketplace role. You have measured the early results, and you regularly stop to celebrate what God is doing through you and your ministry. So are you through Halftime? Not quite.

"How Did I Get Here?"

For many successful people, midlife is the first time they address emotional issues that have been buried on their rush toward accomplishment. The risk at Halftime is to short-circuit the Heart Journey enroute to significance or to confuse these soul issues with our desire to leave a legacy. We run the risk of missing much of the growth and blessing at midlife if we rush off *only* to more accomplishments, even though they may be eternally significant accomplishments.

Perhaps there are four primary seasons of life: struggle, success, significance, and surrender. Our early years are filled with the struggle of getting a good education and landing our first job. Our twenties to mid-forties often are filled with the pursuit of success. Once we begin to achieve some level of success, we begin to see that it will not satisfy and we long for significance. We have dedicated this entire book to the transition between the season of success to the season of significance. But, as we pursue significance by living out God's call on our lives, we realize that the deepest satisfaction comes not so much from accomplishing big things for God (as wonderful as that is) but from surrendering our hearts and agenda to God and living each day in community with him. The Heart Journey at Halftime is about this last issue—letting God change our hearts now that we have loosened our grip on life.

Many of us learn these things best in the trenches of serving alongside God, not sitting at home reading a Bible commentary.

To really understand the Heart Journey of your second half, you must start with a short but quiet reflection on the Heart Journey of your first half. Stop here for a few minutes and ask yourself a few deep questions.

How did I get to where I am, and what was the price along the way?

_____

_____

_____

What drove me to pursue success?

_____

_____

_____

What feelings or needs have I covered up along the way?

_____

_____

_____

In what ways could I live life in fuller color, in the three-dimension of deep intimate relationships and soulfulness?

_____

_____

_____

The Value of the Wilderness

You'll recall that the Bible simply says of Moses that "he fled to Midian, where he settled as a foreigner" (Acts 7:29).

Moses left behind his first-half environment that had provided him with his identity, his security, his sense of belonging, and all the perks that come with being a successful leader. While the wilderness time wasn't comfortable, it did enable God to work on his heart in ways that were essential before he could be used in such a profound world-changing way as he was in his second half.

You may be pushed out of your normal environment by being downsized, through early retirement, or after selling your company. Or you may find yourself still in your normal environment but in an emotional wilderness. You go to the same office every day, but those dreams and rewards that used to captivate you have lost their luster—you find your heart just wandering. It no longer means much that your business card says Director, Partner, or Principal. The corporate goals seem stale.

A friend told me recently that, as his business was growing, he used to love to sit down on Saturday morning and read his own company's advertisements in the city paper. Even though he had helped write those ads, had signed off on the final version, it was very satisfying to see the ads in the paper. But one recent Saturday there was an entire article about a large project his company was building—a front section piece—and he found himself completely uninterested. In fact, he had to admit to his colleagues that he had not read the whole article. He called to ask, "What is wrong with me?"

Nothing is wrong with him, but he is in the wilderness of Halftime. God is weaning him from the things that he clung to for his security and identity. This is a healthy place to be for a short time, but it's not a healthy place to stay.

Risks and Rewards of the Journey

The heart lessons God wants to teach us in Halftime can only occur as we loosen our grip on the things that protect us. Many people who have achieved some level of success in their first half are afraid of failing in new endeavors. The Heart Journey is fraught with the additional risk of being somewhat vague and intangible. Many of the tools that enable people to succeed in their career are not useful in this soul work. Moses was asked by God to put down his staff—which represented his security, income, and identity—to just loosen his grip. Then, as he picked it back up, it became the rod of God and was used in a powerful way in his second half. You too must lay down your staff.

My friend who used to sit down on Saturday mornings to read his own company's ads is now well into this journey. I can already see in his life the rich benefits of living life with a more healthy identity and new measures of performance that are not as tied to the business.

Five Elements of the Heart Journey

Bill Wellons and I have identified five areas where a transformation of the heart occurs: your identity, performance measures, interdependence, intimacy, and servanthood.

1. Your Journey to a New Identity

Many of us are defined by our work, sometimes without even realizing it. Others find their identity defined by other status symbols (titles, awards, their children's accomplishments, how attractive they are) that indicate to them (and perhaps to those around them) that they are of worth. Perhaps you're defined by the sense of having been successful. One of the most devastating occurrences at midlife is when we have this identity stripped away and we come face to face with having to determine who we really are without the title.

My identity is formed when I subconsciously adopt a set of symbols or indicators that define what I feel about myself. When you introduce yourself to someone, what do you instinctively draw on to define who you are? Are those really the things you cling to for identity? A midlife crisis is often triggered when some of these status symbols or markers are taken away from us involuntarily and we're thrust into the messy process of redefining our identity. This can happen if you sell your company, get downsized, retire early, begin to look decidedly older, or if the meaning and value of the things that used to define you dissipate.

Halftime provides us with the opportunity to rethink our identity in a thoughtful, intentional way and reshape an identity grounded on something that will not shake or move.

What truths about you *currently* define your identity? Don't overthink; just write.

a._____

b._____

c._____

What truths about you do you *want* to define your identity?

Before you answer, let me share with you what mine have slowly become: God loves me; I am making an eternal impact in the world using my unique design; I matter deeply to a few people. Whereas, the things that used to define me had to do with my net worth, creating high-class buildings, being focused and aggressive.

Now it's your turn. Write in the three things you feel you most want to define your identity.

a._____

b._____

c._____

Now ask God to help you live out this new identity.

2. Your Development of a New Performance Standard

We often train our hearts to measure our worth and satisfaction based on our performances. Living a life of eternal significance may result in days and years invested in things that are hard to measure. At other times it may appear as if God is squandering our time and talent that we sacrificially give to him.

Psalm 139:16 says, "All the days ordained for [insert your name] were written in your book before one of them came to be." What does this say about God's intentionality in your life and mine?

God has a bigger picture of our lives than our little measures of daily performance. Even as you work hard to make an eternal impact for God through your new ministry, always remember that it is our privilege to partner with God and he reserves the right to determine the results.

3. Your Discovery of the Strength of Interdependence

I loved developing real estate, not only because it's about creating beautiful spaces, but because I loved the independence. As a developer, you decide what land you want to buy, you determine what you want to build, you hire an architect and contractor you like, and you keep the profits. When all was said and done, I always liked walking around the buildings my partner, Andrew Mitton, and I built and feeling a deep sense of satisfaction.

The Heart Journey that accompanies our journey from success to significance involves learning that in the spiritual realm there is an even deeper satisfaction that comes from interdependence—partnering with those people God has uniquely gifted to bring what you simply cannot bring. As I have written this book with Bill, it has been very apparent at times that he brings special abilities and thirty years of ministry experiences that are making this a much more powerful tool.

We spent this past weekend in the quaint little town of Franklin, Tennessee, writing together. Our long hours were a strange mix of fun conversations about life while walking down Main Street looking in the shop windows, intense debate over chapters and stories in a corner of Starbucks, and reflective moments with tears in our eyes as one of us recounted an amazing story of what a Halftimer is doing to serve the Lord. As I drove away from this weekend, I realized we had come to know and love each other at a much deeper level, and I found myself talking to my team about how much spiritual depth, creativity, and wisdom Bill brings to this work. That's the strength of interdependence. What we can offer together is more than the sum of what we could offer independently.

This, to me, is a stunning contrast to the corporate and entrepreneurial self-made ideal that I focused on in my first half.

4. Finding the Confidence to Long for Intimacy

God has always existed in deep, intimate community between the Father, Son, and Spirit. His intent was for us to live in intimacy with him and with one another, but sin created barriers in every direction. Some Christians learn to live in intimacy in their first half. But many of us are so caught up in the pace and pursuit of goals that we have little or no time to understand the value of intimacy or to learn to dismantle the barriers that stand in the way.

Most men arrive at midlife with no really close friendships—I know because I ask them. Every guy I coach through Halftime, I ask about their friendships. As I drill down, I find that nine out of ten men don't really know what it is like to have friends. What happens when we let off the gas in pursuing success is that we realize relationships are not optional; they are essential. A new preoccupation becomes the journey from isolation to intimacy, and it's easier to feel than it is to understand.

Many fear the process because it appears weak. Others fear it because they feel that if God or a few close friends really saw who they were on the inside they'd walk the other way. As we fight being exposed, we miss out on what God has in mind for living out significant second-half lives. The only two things in life that last are the truth of God and relationships. Most of the legacy we are going to leave will occur through being able to draw close to those God brings across our pathway.

5. Seeing the Hero in Being a Servant

Our heroes are most often the strong and valiant, but Jesus gave his followers a different ideal: "You know that the rulers of the Gentiles lord it over them, and their high officials exercise authority over them. Not so with you. Instead, whoever wants to become great among you must be your servant, and whoever wants to be first must be your slave—just as the Son of Man did not come to be served, but to serve, and to give his life as a ransom for many" (Matt. 20:25–28).

We set out on the pursuit of significance—to do something big for God—only to find that this Heart Journey that God will take us on at Halftime moves in the exact opposite direction of our first-half assent up the corporate ladder. Part of the "detox" that we must be prepared for is taking internal steps downward to find deeper satisfaction pursuing significance as a servant.

It's Saturday morning. I drop my daughter Jennie off early for soccer practice and skip over to the bakery shop for breakfast and time to read and reflect. I notice the mentally handicapped man who wipes tables, and as our eyes make contact, I smile, hold the garbage container open for him since his hands are full, and ask him how his day is going. I thank him for the work he is doing. The heroic moments in my inner world now are times like this when I find myself treating a handicapped man who wipes tables with just as much respect as I do the CEOs that I coach through Halftime. These are the changes I most long to see in my heart, even more than accomplishing big things that may be apparent to thousands, and only God can make these heart changes happen.

The Halftimer's Prayer

So what can you do to expedite the Heart Journey? How can you cooperate with the transformation that God desires most and which you secretly long for yourself? Here are two ways:

1. Understand what God is doing so that when it is difficult to swallow, you have a bigger perspective.
2. Pray specifically for God to do this work in your heart. Let me challenge you to shut the door, go on your knees, and pray the Halftimer's Prayer.

"Dear Lord, I am on a journey to find and live out what you placed me on this earth to do. I need your clear direction. I need to see your hand at work and sense your pleasure in what I do. Even more importantly, I want you to transform my heart, even as I partner with you in what you are accomplishing in this universe. Please soften my heart and bring clarity to my thinking so that you can create in me a new identity, a new measurement of my performance, so I become strong through interdependence, enjoy greater intimacy, and live as a servant. Amen."

CHAPTER 10

THE POWER OF ONE STORY

After studying the very latest sources regarding the rise of Christianity in the Roman culture, secular sociologist and author Rodney Stark recently concluded,

> Christianity revitalized life in Greco-Roman cities by providing new norms and new kinds of social relationships able to cope with many urgent urban problems. To cities filled with the homeless and impoverished, Christianity offered charity, as well as hope. To cities filled with newcomers and strangers, Christianity offered an immediate basis for attachments. To cities filled with orphans and widows, Christianity provided a new and expanded sense of family. To cities torn by violence and ethnic strife, Christianity offered a new basis for social solidarity. And to cities faced with epidemics, fires and earthquakes, Christianity offered effective nursing services.[15]

Over the years historians have argued that it was not the Christian theology that prevailed in this era but how they lived. In so doing these historians seek to bypass the living God behind this theology. The obvious second question to their musings is, "What, or more importantly who, gave these people the power to live out a theology that was so radical in its love and sacrifice?" These ideas of loving those outside your family or tribe were unheard of. For a slave to be greeted by a noble as "dear brother" would stop those passing in the street. For the best thinking (and perhaps best think-ers) of the day to go into creating systems to care for hurting people was extraordinary.

This shining moment in church history occurred when God empowered one person, and then another one, to live out their theology. And in so doing he transformed not only the Roman cul-ture but our world today. This power is the power of one person's story—your story.

. Some Next Steps

Because your story matters, over the coming weeks and months we want to help you through your Halftime journey by provid-ing the resources to assist you and your pastor in this partner-ship. The central place to find these and other resources is www .SuccessToSignificance.com. We have listed five possible next steps, beginning with the easiest, yet each fills a different need.

1. Sign up for "My Halftime Guide." This is a free e-mail-based coaching tool that will bring to you the very best ideas, tips, resources, and encouragement to match the stage of Halftime that you are in.

2. Read *From Success to Significance: When the Pursuit of Success Isn't Enough.* This book has helped thousands of people who are not financially independent but wish to pursue significance without leaving their job or selling their company.

3. Bring *Success to Significance* curriculum to your small group. This six-week curriculum will enable your class or small group to process the most important elements of Halftime based on real-life examples. The video stories capture some of the most compelling Halftimers doing the ministry they have been called to. Not only will your group learn from their experiences, and be inspired by them, but the stories will spawn deep, meaningful interaction.

4. Find a Halftime coach. We can connect you with a personal Halftime coach who will work with you one-on-one to support you as you move through this journey.

5. Bring Success to Significance to your church. The *Success to Significance Ministry Guide* provides your church step-by-step advice for partnering with marketplace leaders. It includes easy-to-implement programming elements, curriculum, talks, and compelling video clips to enable everyone in your church (regardless of age and level of success) to pursue significance in their life.

All of these are available at www.SuccessToSignificance.com.

More than a dozen years ago I was faced with a choice—stay focused on making money by developing real estate or open my life to whatever God might have in mind for me for my second half. Because I had achieved a certain level of success, I had options about how I would invest my time and talent in my second half. I knew I would be held accountable. The Bible clearly says, "From everyone who has been given much, much will be demanded" (Luke 12:48).

I took a risk, cut my lifestyle, launched into a space I was not familiar with—but one that used the skills I cultivated as a developer—and tapped into the deep-seated passions that were smoldering in my heart. Along the way there have been days that I wondered if I was making a mistake.

One cold January day I was driving through Toronto, and the sun was setting across Highway 401. Slightly elevated above the city, I could see condos and office buildings being built, cranes high in the air everywhere I turned. It seemed as if there were real estate development signs promoting new buildings across the city on every side. It was a building boom, and I was missing out. Just two years into my journey from success to significance, I was not only missing the thrill of building brand-new buildings from the dirt up,

but at this moment I also had an overwhelming sense that I was getting behind—behind my peers, behind what I could achieve.

The cranes. I could not get them out of my mind. I pulled over and stopped on the side of the highway and quietly asked God to help me trust him that what I felt I was missing out on by not participating in this building boom, he would honor in some eternal way.

I don't often read poetry, much less write it. But in that moment I could not avoid penning this prayer, asking God to give me his sight, his perspective of this short life we live.

Stage Sight
As I cross this stage called "life"
I feel the exhilaration of opportunities rife.
Give me a keen sense of just how fast
This little act of mine will be done—then past.
How can I contemplate God-infinite
And still be absorbed with things so trite?
The exhilaration which opportunity brings

When garnered by God makes my heart sing
Because his Word and Spirit train my sight
So that, in this dark theater, I may reflect a light
So pure and real that it can,
In spite of me, fill the great emptiness of men.
As I dance now in your sight
Keep my feet in step, upright,
And give me a creative, risking mind
For you, and to other opportunities be blind.

—*Lloyd Reeb, January 1995*

Three short years later God gave me the opportunity to build our church campus. As the project came to an end and they took the tall crane away from the site, it dawned on me that I had the privilege to use my skills as a real estate developer to be part of a much bigger and more lasting building boom—the building of the kingdom of God in my community.

As men, women, and children flooded into that building on opening day, I thought about the poem I had written on Highway 401 three years earlier, and in particular the line "Give me a creative, risking mind for you, and to other opportunities be blind." And once again I felt compelled to sit down quietly and write another short poem.

Now I sit in your presence, dear God,
To thank you for your tender prod
To pen that poem and then to see
How you would make it come to be.

The Lord is so clear to us in the Bible when he says, "Let us not become weary in doing good, for at the proper time we will reap a harvest if we do not give up" (Gal. 6:9).

"It is you, O God, who works in me both to will and to do your good pleasure" (Phil. 2:13, paraphrase).

Recap

Today as I reflect back on these years, I am blown away that I have had the privilege of being a part of helping thousands of successful people pursue significance. In fact, it dawned on me that I've had the privilege of being part of the Halftime journey of most of the stories we've talked about in this book:

- James found his niche to launch a men's ministry that has served hundreds of men and through whom some have come to know the Lord.
- Cliff's HopeBuilders ministry now has more than five hundred volunteers, and by partnering with his wife in leading this ministry, it has drawn them closer together.
- Mack led a project through which hundreds heard the gospel and has now begun a second-half journey that we'll have to see where God takes him.
- Lan is bringing all of his talent and resources to lower infant mortality in the Republic of Georgia.
- Joel is exploring three specific ministries right now and has a timeline to select one and give his huge talent full-time to that ministry, for free.
- Ralph is still exploring and that's OK—we are on the journey together.
- Carol is listening carefully to the voice of God, and I believe she has been prepared for a unique role in the lives of at-risk teens in her city.
- Chris is about to launch a third-year campaign to raise the number of AIDS orphans sponsored to more than six hundred children and expand the program to include water supply programs. And this doesn't include how the hearts and lives of each of us who sponsors a child is forever changed through the experience.

And then, to my surprise, I got an e-mail from Chris last week saying:

"I hope you are doing well. I wanted to let you know about a big decision I have made, and solicit your input. I have decided to take early retirement from the bank. (I passed a couple of milestones recently—including my age plus years of service exceeding sixty, which is the retirement rule. That gives me some financial benefit and gives me room for choices.) I have decided to honor the strong pull I feel to invest myself in helping starving children around the world. I plan to combine my long-festering desire to run my own business with my heart's passion to help the chronically poor. I am working on some ideas to start a nonprofit."

- Kenneth is caring for more disabled orphans in China than I will ever know in my lifetime.

Do you think I would trade any one of those stories for all the tea in China?

Today, I am so glad I chose to move from success to significance. And now it's your choice. Take a risk and launch into a second-half adventure that will change the world, one story at a time.

Notes

1. Peter Drucker, "Managing One's Self," *Harvard Business Review*, March–April 1999, executive summary.

2. Rodney Stark, *The Rise of Christianity* (Princeton, N.J.: Princeton University Press, 1966), 3.

3. William H. McNeill, *Plagues and Peoples* (New York: Anchor Press/Doubleday, 1976), 116.

4. Dionysius, quoted in Stark, *The Rise of Christianity*, 82.

5. Paul Johnson, *A History of Christianity* (New York: Simon & Schuster, 1976), 75.

6. E-mail from Karen Jo Torjesen to Bob Buford, January 2006.

7. Stark, *The Rise of Christianity*, 7.

8. MetLife Foundation/Civic Ventures, "New Face of Work Study," June 2005, page 7. Also *Reinventing Aging: Baby Boomers and Civic Engagement* (Boston: Harvard School of Public Health-MetLife Foundation, 2004), 3.

9. MetLife Foundation/Civic Ventures report, 7.

10. Richard Conniff, "Are You Happy?" *Men's Health*, January–February 2006.

11. MetLife Foundation/Civic Ventures report.

12. Elements of these four stages have been excerpted from *From Success to Significance* (Grand Rapids: Zondervan, 2004).

13. Jim Collins, "Good to Great and the Social Sector," a monograph to accompany *Good to Great*, self-published by Jim Collins, p. 5, date unknown.

14. Ken Blanchard and Phil Hodges, *Lead Like Jesus* (Nashville: W Publishing Group, 2006).

15. Stark, *The Rise of Christianity*, 161.

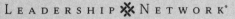

"At last, a book that bridges the gap between gifted layleaders and pastors. We are often like two different breeds speaking two different dialects but with a common passion for serving Christ. Here's a lexicon of terms and behaviors that will connect leaders and pastors and unleash their energies for transforming the world."

Dave Peterson—Senior Pastor
Memorial Drive Presbyterian Church,
Houston, TX (partnering with Peter Forbes,
Former CFO, Fund-raising Director for
Louis Palau's Cityfest Houston)

"This approach may be new turf for many churches, but it offers solid long-term payoffs. We have to remind ourselves that there is risk in controlling people just as there is risk in letting people loose. I firmly believe that the risk in not doing is greater than the risk of doing."

Wade Paschal—Senior Pastor
First United Methodist Church, Tulsa, OK
(partnering with Clark Millspaugh, President
of Summit Exploration, LLC; Director of
Men's Ministry at FUMC Tulsa)

"Halftime is 'hidden in plain sight' from most pastors. Who better than Bill Wellons and Lloyd Reeb to build the vision? Church is one of the venues to act as a platform for significance. I can only imagine what the potential is ten years from now."

Bob Buford—Author of
Halftime and *Finishing Well*,
Founder of Leadership Network

UNLIMITED
PARTNERSHIP

UNLIMITED
PARTNERSHIP

IGNITING A MARKETPLACE LEADER'S
JOURNEY TO SIGNIFICANCE

PASTOR'S EDITION

BILL WELLONS LLOYD REEB

PUBLISHING GROUP

NASHVILLE, TENNESSEE

ISBN: 978-0-8054-4450-6

Published by B & H Publishing Group,
Nashville, Tennessee

Dewey: 253.7
Subject Heading: MINISTRY \ EVANGELISTIC WORK
                 CHURCH WORK WITH COMMUNITY

Unless otherwise designated, Scripture quotations are from the New American Standard
Bible, copyright © 1960, 1962, 1963, 1968, 1971, 1972, 1973, 1975, 1977, 1995 by The
Lockman Foundation.

10 9 8 7 6 5 4 3 2 1   10 09 08 07 06

Contents

To the Elders
of Fellowship Bible Church in Little Rock, Arkansas.
Your partnership with me is a special gift from the Lord because
you are more than great churchmen—you are Kingdom Builders!
Thank you for empowering me to do what I do best.
I love you guys.

Foreword

Agrowing number of seasoned business leaders (often called Halftimers) want to use their skills and experience to make a difference for the Lord in their world—and the obvious place for doing so is through their church. But many feel stuck. They have no idea where to begin or who to talk to.

At the same time, pastors and church leaders long for their churches to make an even greater impact for Christ in their communities and around the world, but they lack the seasoned leaders and ministry model necessary to make it happen.

What is desperately needed *now* is a way to join these two groups of people together to unleash the kingdom power that such a partnership can provide.

This unique flip-book does that. Read it forward to understand the perspective and challenges facing a pastor. Flip it over to comprehend the perspective and issues facing a business leader. Both viewpoints have been written to bridge the gap and exploit the spiritual potential that exists between high-capacity leaders and kingdom-minded pastors.

Whether you are a church leader or marketplace leader, let me invite you to read both viewpoints. Then you will be ready to develop a partnership with unlimited potential for spiritual influence. King Solomon, the wisest man to ever live, once said, "Two are better than one because they have a good return for their labor"

(Eccles. 4:9). I believe you will find a new power of "two together" in the pages of this book.

Both sides of this partnership are practical and relevant, filled with compelling real-life stories of business leaders and pastors who are connecting for the first time to make a leveraged impact for God's kingdom. These stories will not only inspire you; they will challenge you to the core.

The Halftime movement is a growing phenomenon. It simply did not exist in previous generations. It is a new movement of God representing unprecedented opportunities for the church. Pastors, please don't miss this opportunity to empower and release the business leaders of your church for greater kingdom impact. And business leaders, please don't turn your back on the prompting of God in your heart to leverage your skills and experiences for eternal significance. There is a thrilling adventure out there for both of you when you are willing to trust God for this ministry partnership.

As founder and teaching pastor of a large church for more than thirty years, Bill Wellons has led the way by methodically finding and engaging Halftimers to serve both inside and outside his church. Having served with Bill personally, I know firsthand that he brings to his writing a host of proven practices from this wealth of experience.

As a successful real estate developer and business leader, Lloyd Reeb shares his own personal journey from success to significance. God is now using Lloyd as the national spokesperson for Halftime as well as the pastor of leadership development for his church. Lloyd uniquely brings the business leader's perspective to kingdom work, along with a sense of unwavering optimism for his peers.

These men long to help pastors and marketplace leaders lock arms as partners to courageously advance the kingdom of God together. Together is *always* better.

Dr. Robert M. Lewis
Author, *The Church of Irresistible Influence*
Founder of Men's Fraternity

CHAPTER 1

THE NEW SOCIAL MOVEMENT

Social Movement—"A group of people
with a common ideology who try to achieve certain goals."
(Encyclopedia Britannica)

An exciting social movement is brewing that will bring an unprecedented surge of new, seasoned leaders and their resources into your ministry. The question is not "if" or "when" they are coming but "how" they will be identified, challenged, equipped, and unleashed to serve.

Bob Buford, Christian philanthropist and founder of Leadership Network, has labeled this new social movement the Halftime Phenomenon. He characterizes Halftime as a pause at life's midpoint to reflect upon what you have accomplished and who you have become. It is an opportunity for reassessing the course of your life and choosing to reinvest it in more meaningful ways.

These so-called Halftimers are likely packing your pews. They represent a seasoned group of high-capacity leaders, both male and female, who have refined skills and abilities, leadership savvy, spiritual maturity, time, and financial resources. As a pastor, you have the opportunity to help guide these Halftimers on their soul-searching journey.

What is this unprecedented group of people in your church going to be challenged to do with their bonus years? Are there

1

adjustments to your ministry mind-set and church structure that need to be considered? Is your church ready to catch this wave of opportunity and maximize it for God's glory? If a Halftimer came to you and asked for help in finding a ministry that fit their God-given design, would you know what to say? What might God accomplish if just one partnership was forged between a pastor and a Halftimer in every church across America and around the world?

I found out what could happen through one special partnership. I'll tell you more about that later in this chapter, but first let's consider both the history and contemporary implication of social movements.

The power of a social movement to bring about radical changes in values and way of life is unmistakable. Throughout history, societal reform thought impossible by one generation is realized by another generation. Two well-known, twentieth-century social movements speak to this reality.

The American Civil Rights Movement of the 1960s, demanding civil rights and equality under the law to all Americans, regardless of race, is a dramatic example. Who would have thought that Rosa Parks' refusal to give up her seat on a bus to make room for white people would have sparked such significant reform?

In the 1980s, another well-known social movement developed after trade union activist Anna Walentynowicz was fired from work. The resulting Polish Solidarity movement proved to be the critical factor in the downfall of the communist regimes of Eastern Europe. Open doors to capitalism and democracy followed. Former generations would not have considered change of this magnitude possible!

Four Essential Ingredients

There are four essential ingredients in social movements such as these that generate incredible changes in values and way of life. A social movement is when a *multitude* of people, at a unique *moment*

in history, with a common *mission*, experience greater *meaning* in their lives.

Think about it. Whether the issue is civil rights or political reform, these four—multitude, moment, mission, and meaning—are all present. Evaluate any major social movement and you will find these ingredients in the mix, producing previously unthinkable changes.

With this in mind, let's turn the historical clock back several hundred years and take a brief look at the greatest social movement of all. The lasting changes in values and way of life that it influenced could never have been foreseen. It started and flourished during a most unlikely moment in history, under the rule of the Roman Empire.

The name of this social movement is the rise of Christianity.

Historian Will Durant says of the rise of Christianity as a social movement, "There is no greater drama in human record than the sight of a few Christians, scorned or oppressed by a succession of emperors, bearing all trials with a fierce tenacity, multiplying quietly, building order while their enemies generate chaos, fighting the sword with the word, brutality with hope and at last defeating the strongest state that history has known. Caesar and Christ had met in the arena, and Christ had won."[1]

The overwhelming success of this movement raises a great question. As sociologist Rodney Stark puts it, "How did a tiny and obscure messianic movement from the edge of the Roman Empire dislodge classical paganism and become the dominant faith of Western Civilization?"[2] How was this possible?

As in our day, there were macro social and economic factors that made this social movement possible. The Roman Empire had established peace, roads, common language, and other such factors that aided the spread of Christianity, and most historians agree that early persecution actually benefited the rise of Christianity. Without persecution, the members of the first church might have stayed in Jerusalem indefinitely. As Tertullian once said, "The blood of the martyrs is the seed of the Church."

One overwhelmingly difficult moment in this time period when Christianity as a social movement proved its mettle arrived during the great epidemic that struck the Roman world around AD 260. At its height, five thousand people a day were reported to have died in the city of Rome alone.[3] How did this growing *multitude* of Christians respond at this unique *moment* in history? What was their common *mission,* and how did it add greater *meaning* and a sense of purpose to their lives?

Acknowledging the enormous death rate, Dionysius, bishop of Alexandria, wrote a lengthy tribute to the heroic nursing efforts of local Christians, many of whom lost their lives caring for others during this epidemic.

> Most of our brother Christians showed unbounded love and loyalty, never sparing themselves and thinking only of one another. Heedless of danger, they took charge of the sick, attending to their every need and ministering to them in Christ, and with them departed this life serenely happy; for they were infected by others with the disease, drawing on themselves the sickness of their neighbors and cheerfully accepting their pains. Many, in nursing and curing others, transferred their death to themselves and died in their stead. . . . The best of our brothers lost their lives in this manner, a number of presbyters, deacons, and laymen winning high commendation so that death in this form, the result of great piety and strong faith, seems in every way the equal of martyrdom.[4]

At a time when pagan faiths were found lacking, Christianity offered explanation and comfort. More importantly, Christian doctrine provided a prescription for action: "It is more blessed to give than to receive." Christians wanted to serve others by showing compassion for them because this is how they had been loved by God. "For while we were still helpless, at the right time Christ died for the ungodly" (Rom. 5:6).

Evidence even from pagan resources confirms that this was characteristic Christian behavior. A century later the emperor Julian, who loathed Christians, launched a campaign to institute pagan charities to match the Christians. He complained in a letter to the high priest of Galatia in 362 that the pagans needed to somehow equal the virtues of Christians, for recent Christian growth was caused by their "moral character, even if pretended," and by their "benevolence toward strangers and care for the graves of the dead." He also wrote, "[T]he impious Galileans support not only their poor, but ours as well, everyone can see that our people lack aid from us."[5]

Simply stated, a social movement was generating unthinkable changes in values and ways of life. Christians were penetrating the world with the love of Christ by living out what they claimed they believed.

Now, let's return to our four ingredients:

A multitude of people — in this case, Christians. Sociologist Rodney Stark estimates six million by AD 300.[6]

At a unique moment in history — the first three hundred to four hundred years after the death and resurrection of Jesus Christ, under Roman rule.

With a common mission — to penetrate the world with the sacrificial love of Christ. Christians wanted to please their God by serving the needs of others in the manner that they had been served by their Savior. "For even the Son of Man did not come to be served, but to serve, and to give His life a ransom for many" (Mark 10:45).

Experience greater meaning in their lives. These Christ-followers enjoyed the privilege of partnering with God. They gave their lives to benefit others, and it felt significant to them because it *was* significant. Their lives had a clear purpose—and it was not about them.

The change-producing power of a multitude of Christ-followers motivated by God to invest their time, talent, and treasure to benefit the world in which they live is beyond human

comprehension. Imagine what it would be like if there were a new social movement in the twenty-first century that was similar in life-changing impact to this social movement of the first century.

Is it conceivable that what former generations believed impossible could be realized in our generation? Can a Christian be a difference-maker for God in our culture? Is it possible for the church of Jesus Christ to be admired and appreciated by those in our communities who are presently critical and hostile toward us?

Researcher George Barna says, "[T]he stumbling block for the Church is not its theology but its failure to apply what it believes in compelling ways. . . . Christians have been their own worst enemies when it comes to showing the world what authentic, biblical Christianity looks like."[7]

But at this unique moment in time, is God providing a new wave of opportunity to build his kingdom? Lloyd Reeb and I believe the answer to that question is a resounding "Yes!"

Another Perfect Storm

In October 1991, a storm developed off the eastern seaboard from a collision between three critical factors: a high pressure system, a low pressure system, and the remnants from dying Hurricane Grace. The National Weather Service named this unprecedented, monster storm "the perfect storm." Its power sent high winds and Atlantic Ocean waves crashing into the East Coast from New England to Cape Hatteras, North Carolina.

I believe, as do others, that another perfect storm is developing—an equally unprecedented storm of opportunity where certain sociological factors are coming together at just the right time to unleash great power and energy for good. Many are unaware of this new social phenomenon and the challenges and opportunities that it offers.

Peter Drucker, the father of modern management and author of more than thirty books, states in a *Leader to Leader* article, "In a few hundred years, when the history of our time will be written

from a long-term perspective, it is likely that the most important event historians will see is not technology, not the internet, not e-commerce. It is an unprecedented change in the human condition. For the first time—literally—substantial and rapidly growing numbers of people have choices. For the first time, they will have to manage themselves. And society is totally unprepared for it."[8]

The sociological factors behind this unprecedented change in the human condition that Drucker is describing are: *longevity, the demographics and mind-set of "baby boomers,"* and *affluence.* All three are converging at just the right moment in history. Storm clouds are forming to create the perfect environmental conditions for a powerful social movement.

Consider the facts. In 1900, the average life span was below fifty years of age. In 2005, a great majority of people in one-third of the developed world can anticipate active, healthy, productive living to eighty years of age and beyond. For the first time, we now have thirty bonus years!

The unprecedented change is that large numbers of people, a growing *multitude,* have choices about how they will invest and leverage their bonus years.

Drucker confirms, "Demographics will be the most important factor in the next society."[9] "Second careers" and the "second half" of one's life have become buzz words in America. Increasingly, men and women take early retirement but do not stop working. These "second careers" often will take unconventional forms.

The MetLife Foundation/Civic Ventures' "New Face of Work" survey findings in April 2005 constitute the first in-depth look at the pre-boomers and leading-edge boomers' priorities for the next stage of work. Questions explored in their research included:

- What kind of work does the current and coming generation of Americans in their fifties and sixties actually want to do?
- What are these individuals looking to accomplish through work after the traditional working years?

- Do these priorities fit with where we are likely to need people?
- Is there a great disjuncture between what the new generation of aging workers wants and what the economy and society need?

Research Summary

Indicators point to fresh opportunities of staggering proportions for making a difference. The summary facts of the survey are:

1. *Half of all Americans age fifty to seventy want work that helps others.* A full 50 percent are interested in taking jobs now and in retirement that help improve the quality of life in their communities. What kind of work do they want to do?

- More than three-quarters (78 percent) are interested in working to help the poor, the elderly, and other people in need.
- Fifty-six percent are interested in dealing with health issues, whether working in a hospital or with an organization fighting a particular disease.
- Fifty-five percent are interested in teaching or other educational positions.
- Forty-five percent say they are interested in working in a youth program.[10]

2. *Second careers in the retirement years are about people, purpose, and community.* When specifically asked, "Why do you (Americans fifty to seventy) want to continue working in retirement?" this is how they responded:

- Six in ten (59 percent) say staying involved with other people is very important in attracting them to a job in retirement.
- Fifty-seven percent say the job gives them a sense of purpose.
- About half (52 percent) say the job provides additional income.

- And nearly half (48 percent) say the job provides the opportunity to help improve the quality of life in their community.[11]

Interestingly, women boomers top the list, with 70 percent of females age fifty to fifty-nine saying it is very important that a job in retirement gives them a sense of purpose.

3. *Nearly half (48 percent) of Americans age fifty to seventy think it may be difficult to find good work.* Could the church of Jesus Christ become the place to help people discover what God has designed them to do and to find their best-fit, inside or outside the church, serving the needs of others? (See Matt. 5:16.)

The MetLife Research observes, "This drive contains many of the features of a social movement." Sound familiar? A social movement is when a *multitude* of people, at a unique *moment* in history, experience greater *meaning* in their lives, while pursuing a common *mission.*

A multitude of people . . . A 2003 report estimates that approximately 77 million babies were born in the United States during the boom years of 1946 to 1964. In 2011, the oldest will turn sixty-five and, on average, can expect to live to eighty-three.[12]

. . . *at a unique moment in history*—At the convergence of longevity, unusual boomer demographics, and affluence—at this very moment and into the twenty-second century—could others follow in the footsteps of the boomers to change the world?

. . . *pursuing a common mission*—A heartfelt desire to serve people and improve the quality of life in their communities is a strong motivator.

. . . *to experience greater meaning in their lives*—For Christians, this opportunity affords new ways to partner with God, using the unique gifts and abilities he has given them to penetrate the world with the love of Jesus Christ (Eph. 2:10).

Now, back to my story of a special partnership.

In July 2000, this Halftime phenomenon and its exciting possibilities for our church were weighing on my mind as my wife

Carolyn and I went away for a three-week sabbatical from my ministry responsibilities at Fellowship Bible Church in Little Rock. We spent some much-needed, uninterrupted downtime at a friend's cabin on a beautiful lake in Arkansas. Interestingly, I was fifty-one at the time. During our stay, we set aside one particular day for personal prayer, planning, and dreaming about our future ministry. I can still see myself seated alone at a small table, asking God to direct my future contributions to his kingdom. During this prayer time, I experienced a certain inner stirring of my heart to begin a discipleship ministry to men who, like me, were experiencing the Halftime phenomenon that I just described.

I had no idea how I was going to go about this, but from numerous conversations with men in our church, I knew I was on the right track. They all made similar comments about having "an inner itch" to do something more meaningful or significant for God. They wanted to leverage their learning from the first part of their lives in the second part but didn't know how to go about it (and neither did I at that time). The Lord brought to mind the names of five men that day, and I wrote them down on a sheet of paper.

When I returned home, I challenged each man individually to join me for one year to process our Halftime journeys together. One hundred percent said yes! Among this group was my close friend and fellow elder, Tom. Unbeknownst to me, Tom had an experience with the Lord similar to mine just prior to my challenge. It began a very special partnership in ministry that continues to this day. I asked Tom to describe his Halftime journey to you.

Tom's Story

During my collegiate experience, I learned to work hard to achieve results, but I also began on a path of following Jesus Christ in a very real way. Those tracks were to parallel one another and overlap throughout my career. Never mutually exclusive, I knew instinctively my spiritual walk had to be integrated into my professional pursuits.

My professional journey led from a family manufacturing business to graduate school to the sale of that business, and then to a twenty-five-year financial advisory career. Along the way, I learned much about finance, consulting, presentation, and analysis. I met with success at various points professionally. I learned much about life and myself.

As my professional path evolved, so did my spiritual trek. All along the way, I held on to a clear commitment to follow Christ in each circumstance. At many points, translating that into action was not simple, but I found many opportunities to touch those around me through the journey while serving in numerous capacities through my church in Little Rock. As I spread my professional wings, I also tested my spiritual gifts.

In the late 1990s, I sensed a stirring inside me to carve out a portion of the energy and time I was pouring into my business to focus in a greater way with eternity in my sights. The satisfaction of professional success was palpable, but it was never "enough" nor a satisfying end in itself. As I saw new vistas opening for our church as we began looking beyond our walls to serve others and the larger body of Christ in a more deliberate manner, I felt the same desire personally to serve Christ and contribute in a different, more purposeful way. I had no idea what that meant practically. I had even less of an idea how to address that stirring.

At this point in life, my wife and I had four relatively young daughters. We were not independently wealthy, and I could see ahead far enough to predict significant expenses on the horizon. The question of finances was very real. At the same time, so was the "itch" that was growing in my heart. I began to pray, talk with my wife, and counsel with my pastors and a few trusted advisors. Mostly

I prayed, read, and sought God. My time in this "desert process" spanned a few years but was most intense for the first half of 2000. I felt a great tension between being in my years of highest earning capacity with the attendant sense of security and my heart-level sense that it was time to go to a new place of giving more of myself away for the eternal. An internal struggle ensued.

There was no burning bush in my story where God spoke audibly, giving direction. As I pursued him during this period, I asked many, many questions. I took time alone to process. I sought wise counsel to determine if this was simply some variety of midlife crisis. Along the way, God was gracious to send several relevant books across my path that were extremely helpful. My wife was patient and kind in allowing room to process, although any new direction held significant implications for our family. My spiritual counselors were invaluable in their comments and insights. At each turn, God gently addressed my questions and concerns. At times I felt a bit overwhelmed, even startled by the clarity of his answers. I became confident in his leading to move ahead in making some changes.

The culmination of the process came when I felt a need to communicate with my business partners during planning for the upcoming year. My wife's encouragement at that moment was to communicate with them my decision to rebalance my life. We were moving from the realm of theory to reality, thus drawing a "line in the sand" for me. The next day I presented my desires to my partners. We negotiated my time and flexibility up, and my income down. They were quite supportive and generous. I was relieved, but then the question of "what now?" hit me right between the eyes.

At lunch with Bill Wellons, one of my pastors, he

shared his interest in getting a small group of men together to process these exact questions about life, balance, and direction for the "second half." I eagerly joined, and we spent several months exploring our unique God-given design, experience, and gifting, and how we might answer his call in our lives at the moment. This proved to be exactly the right help at the right time. We shared our hearts honestly and, in that small community, each of us found help and direction for the next steps in our unique journey. I am grateful I was not left to myself to process these next steps alone.

Since rebalancing my energy and time, I have been surprised by some of the realities. First, through the small group process I decided my wife and children needed more of me than I was giving. Stepping away from the drive of marketplace success to coach a girls' soccer team has been a joyful thing, although not as simple emotionally as it may sound. Planning family times and vacations may have always been on your schedule, but I fell far short in that and other categories. I find I now have energy to do those things. I did not realize how little of me was really left at the end of the day.

Not putting on a suit and tie every day is disorienting. Years of "knowing what to do" have been replaced with learning to look around me to see God working and to join him there. That is a new "way of seeing" that I am cultivating.

I am now partnering with Bill, serving others in this transition process; helping lead our church to be prepared for the waves of baby boomers crashing headlong into these issues; spending more time serving in church leadership; initiating intentional mentoring relationships with younger men; and reaching out to rural churches to give away some of the resources God has given our church.

Tom (second from right) with Halftimers

Is the "itch" to serve God satisfied? No. I don't expect it to ever go away. I believe what I am feeling is the itch to live by faith in a new way. Maybe God will do "big" things through me, who knows? Right now I know clearly that my wife and daughters love seeing dad on the field being a part of life today. I welcome the opportunities to meet with a new acquaintance for lunch to talk about this "itch" he has that he can't quite articulate. That's enough for me. I wouldn't trade it for anything!

And I wouldn't trade Tom for anything either! He is a multi-talented leader whom God is using to minister deeply in the lives of others. This year I challenged him to assume the day-to-day oversight of the Halftime ministry at our church that we call Kingdom Builders. He accepted. He plans and helps me lead workshops for other churches, launches new small groups of Halftimers, coaches the leaders of these groups, and will part-ner again with me to teach on Halftime at our National Church Conference.

More importantly, Tom cheers for me to win and I cheer for him. We want to help each other maximize who we are for the glory

of God. Tom and I have enjoyed numerous open, honest conversations about every conceivable aspect of our Christian lives. We discuss who should lead what and why, based on our God-given designs. We seek the Lord's vision for our ministry each year and establish plans for it together. He is a great team player. We have discovered the simple truth that doing ministry together is far better than doing ministry alone.

Tom is representative of a growing *multitude* of people, baby boomers, at our unique *moment* in history, with a common *mission,* "an inner itch" to be used by God and do more for his kingdom, who are experiencing greater *meaning* in their lives as they discover their unique abilities and giftings and find their fit in service both inside and outside the church.

So where do we go from here? In the following chapters, Lloyd and I will answer the most frequently asked questions that have surfaced from our research—questions like:

- Are there some predictable stages in this journey that a Halftimer experiences?
- How do pastors go about identifying Halftimers in their church?
- What can church leaders do to help Halftimers assess their gifts and abilities and find their best-fit in service?
- What issues do Halftimers need coaching in after they start their new endeavors?
- Where can a pastor go to learn more about Halftime tools and resources?

Step by step, we will walk you through a "how-to" field manual that will equip you to get started, one partnership at a time.

CHAPTER 2

UNDERSTANDING THE UNIQUE STAGES OF HALFTIME

M ike's professional life as an attorney for the federal government and as a JAG officer in the Air National Guard had been a good fit for him and his family, but by his own admission, he was "tired." He was fifty-five years old and eligible for retirement. He could walk out the door of his legal career at any time; however, if he worked just five more years, his retirement pay would increase significantly. But Mike had an inner desire for more than money. In fact, he had drafted a personal mission statement a few years earlier that said he wanted to serve the Lord in a second career, in a significant role that fit his God-given design and experience. He wanted to invest his time, talent, and treasure in his bonus years in something different, but he didn't know what that was.

That's when the phone rang.

"A phone call from your pastor at 9 p.m.," says Mike, "is usually not good news. But this call was life-changing for the good." I called Mike to challenge him to pray about retiring earlier than he had planned in order to assume a full-time staff position partnering with me at our church. Of course, he would have to take a cut in pay, but the role was an exciting one. Mike had been in a class I taught called "Your Unique Design," where he learned about God's handiwork in his life and that God had special work

for him to do (Eph. 2:10). His completion of the assessment tool we use called the "Servants By Design™ Inventory" (www.your uniquedesign.com) and our interaction over his results led me to make the call. I was asking Mike to be a construction manager and owner's representative for a new multimillion-dollar student center that the church was planning to build and oversee the care and maintenance of our existing facilities. I knew he had a good deal of experience in contract law and that he and his wife had built two houses and remodeled several others. As a Christ-follower, he is known as a man of utmost integrity.

Mike Celebrating Finished Project

Mike says, "That call was a real wake-up for me. My heart leaped in my chest as Bill described this position. Is this what I had been waiting for all these years?" Mike said yes, and seven years later he has overseen millions of dollars in construction and given leadership to our campus operations with excellence.

Listen to Mike, as he speaks from experience: "Stepping out in faith and accepting this role gave greater meaning and significance to my life. I knew that God had designed this opportunity and prepared me for it through my first-half experience. When you get the call, I encourage you to say yes. Believe me; you will be glad you did."

Halftime by its very nature is not a program, not an event, nor a decision. Rather, it is a process or journey. There are two important tracks to this journey:

1. *The Head Journey*—This track involves a pause at life's midpoint to reflect upon what you have accomplished and who you have become. It is an opportunity for reassessing the course of your life and choosing to reinvest it in a best-fit serving role that you discover.

2. *The Heart Journey*—This track involves what the Lord wants to do in your soul as he leads you through Halftime. It is about redefining success and pursuing significance.

The Head Journey requires: discovering who you are at the **Core** (your God-given design, strengths, and passions), creating **Capacity** or time to begin giving yourself away, and identifying the ultimate serving **Context** that fits you (the environment, the role, type of ministry, etc.).

Mike had to address all three—core, capacity, and context—to make the midlife transition that he made. It was a process for him and every person who experiences the Halftime phenomenon.

Let's take a deeper look at the stages of this process. As pastors, we need to understand this if we are going to help our Halftimers find their niche in building God's kingdom.

The Stages of Halftime

The life of Moses is an excellent example of an Old Testament Halftimer. Dwight L. Moody, writing about Moses' journey, once said, "Moses spent his first forty years thinking he was a somebody. He spent his second forty years learning he was a nobody. He spent his third forty years discovering what God can do with a nobody."[13]

I think that's a pretty good description of what a Halftimer experiences. Moody highlights the fact that there are some identifiable stages to the Halftime phenomenon. What are these stages?

What is going on in a person's life in each stage? An examination of Moses' Halftime experience answers these questions.

In Acts chapter 7, beginning at verse 17, the Bible gives us God's overview of Moses' life:

> But as the time of the promise was approaching which God had assured to Abraham, the people increased and multiplied in Egypt, until THERE AROSE ANOTHER KING OVER EGYPT WHO KNEW NOTHING ABOUT JOSEPH. It was he who took shrewd advantage of our race and mistreated our fathers so that they would expose their infants and they would not survive. It was at this time that Moses was born; and he was lovely in the sight of God, and he was nurtured three months in his father's home. And after he had been set outside, Pharaoh's daughter took him away and nurtured him as her own son. Moses was educated in all the learning of the Egyptians, and he was a man of power in words and deeds. (Acts 7:17–22)

FOUNDATION™

OF SUCCESS

Stage One: Foundation of Success

This first stage in Moses' journey is called the "Foundation of Success." In twenty-first-century language, he spent his first forty years in Pharaoh's court getting his master's degree and climbing the corporate ladder. He came to understand the system that drove Egyptian politics. He learned leadership skills and refined his people skills, which served him well later in life. I am sure that this seemed like the most important season of his life. But in reality, these first forty years were only a platform. A foundation of success was being laid that God would use to build a second half of eternal significance.

Acts chapter 7 goes on to say this about Moses: "But when he was approaching the age of forty, it entered his mind to visit his brethren, the sons of Israel. And when he saw one of them being treated unjustly, he defended him and took vengeance for the

oppressed by striking down the Egyptian. And he supposed that his brethren understood that God was granting them deliverance through him, but they did not understand" (Acts 7:23–25).

At midlife, something tugged at Moses' heartstrings. He had achieved success, status, and power. But he began thinking, *Is this all there is? Is this what I was placed on earth to do?* He began searching for something more. I believe he was experiencing the beginning of Halftime.

He walked out of Pharaoh's court one day into his community with a new perspective: he was overwhelmed by his people's pain, their suffering, and their needs. Something inside him exploded.

This internal explosion was a unique passion God had placed in his heart to make a difference in his world by freeing his people from bondage. It was as if he had stepped off the corporate treadmill of business, stress, and responsibility to discover a greater purpose for his life. He came alive. He was energized. At that very moment, Moses was getting in touch with why God placed him on the planet.

I wish a pastor had been there to partner with Moses and coach him about how to address the needs of his community. Unfortunately, he defaulted to his top-down power approach to problem-solving, and it didn't work. Frustrated by the circumstances, he lost his temper and killed the Egyptian who was abusing one of his people.

It seemed so apparent to him that he could use his position of power and influence to change Israel's plight. He thought others would see that he was called to free his people, but they did not.

Instead they said, "Who made you a ruler and judge over us? You do not mean to kill me as you killed the Egyptian yesterday, do you?" (Acts 7:27–28).

Moses' intentions were good; his approach was not. Regardless, the first half of his life was not wasted. It was a valuable time of preparation. An important foundation had been laid, but before he could begin to be used by God in his second half, he needed time

for reflection and some soul-searching. He needed time to process some of the heart aspects of his journey.

The Bible says, "Moses fled, and became an alien in the land of Midian" (Acts 7:29).

JOURNEY™

Stage Two: Journey Inward

Moses was now entering a second stage of Halftime called the "Journey Inward." He was confused and frightened. The solitude of the desert would prove to be perfect for his season of unrest INWARD and introspection. He had been a somebody in Egypt; now he was a nobody, a foreigner. God was going to use this forty-year period to detox Moses of some of the baggage of his first half so that he could use him to make an eternal impact in his second half. A lesson he learned was that his real identity was not found in a position of power, but only in his personal relationship with God. Moses had been humbled by his failure in Egypt, and as a result his heart was more open to listen for God's plan and calling on his life.

After Linda's last child entered elementary school, she took a part-time job as a project manager in a communications department. Though she enjoyed the people and her supervisor was pleased with her work, she sensed that she was wasting her time and talent. She says, "Two years into the job, I began a soul-searching journey that would change everything. Questions without answers plagued me. Who am I, and how does God want to use me to contribute to his kingdom? What am I uniquely gifted to do? And what did Paul mean when he told his young protégé Timothy, 'Take hold of the eternal life to which you have been called, that which is life indeed.' What is life indeed?"

Like Moses, Linda was experiencing the journey inward. Halftimers need encouragement and guidance during this stage. They need resources to read, people around to help sort out their confusion, and examples of what others are doing in their second half. If married, they need to be exhorted to include their spouse in

the journey without scaring him or her with a surprise announcement like, "I quit my job today, honey, and we're going to Africa!"

One challenging aspect of this stage for me was processing with my wife Carolyn my own transition from being a teaching pastor of nearly thirty years to executive director of church planting and consulting. As you might imagine, this was quite an adjustment for her. Not only was my identity changing, but hers would be impacted as well. My transition represented a change from being up front and public as a teaching pastor to more behind-the-scenes and private as a consultant and mentor to young pastors. Had I not heard the "still small voice of God" during my own desert experience, I could never have made this move for second-half impact. Had I not had other godly men to pray for me and counsel me confirming my gifting and calling, I might still be confused. And had Carolyn and I not prayed about this and processed it together under the Lord's leadership, I think we might still be struggling through it. Thankfully, God knew all along that we would end up partnering in ministry to these church-planting couples, with me mentoring the men and Carolyn the women. It is the most exciting thing we have ever done in ministry together.

This journey inward stage of Halftime is not something you rush through. God is working to help the Halftimer redefine success in the first half in favor of pursuing significance in the second. It is hard work because it is heart work.

The Bible continues, "After forty years passed, an angel appeared to him in the wilderness of Mount Sinai, in the flame of a burning thorn bush. . . . [Then the Lord said,] 'Come now, and I will send you to Egypt'" (Acts 7:30–34).

Stage Three: Awakening Challenge

What a wake-up call this must have been for Moses! God was speaking to him, saying "Let's partner together to set the nation of Israel free from slavery." His assignment fit the skills and

AWAKENING

CHALLENGE

abilities that God had given him. It was consistent with the passion that the Lord had hardwired into him. But it still required risk, faith, and sacrifice. Keep in mind that his first attempt at being the deliverer had not gone well. Appropriately, this stage is called "Awakening Challenge."

Obviously, every Halftimer does not have a burning bush experience. But they all are very concerned with discovering their *Core* (God-given design, strengths, and passions), their *Capacity* (how they will create time to begin giving themselves away), and their serving *Context* (the environment, the role, and the ministry they will perform).

All Halftimers wonder how to make their highest and best contribution. Some find their best-fit back in the marketplace or inside the walls of their *church*. Others discover a unique passion for serving a need in their *community*. Still others are led to minister in another *country* altogether.

Regardless, people in Halftime need the partnership of their pastor to explore these issues with them, to pray with them for God's leadership in their lives, and to assist them in finding their niche in building God's kingdom (Eph. 4:11–12).

Two years ago, I met Bill when he showed up with a few friends to help Carolyn and me move from our home of twenty-four years. He was fairly new to our church, so I asked him to join me for lunch the following week. There I learned that Bill was a registered engineer who had retired recently from a successful first-half career as a senior vice-president for Lucent Technologies. He wasn't sure about how he was going to invest his time, talent, and treasure in his future, but he was sure he wanted to serve people and honor the Lord in doing so.

I asked him to join my Kingdom Builders group, and he agreed. This is a small group that I lead with Halftimers to help them discover service opportunities that match their skills, abilities, and passion. Over the next several months, I learned a lot about Bill's organizational and problem-solving skills, and became aware of his

amazing abilities in relational networking. He also shared his passion for the inner city; that he was mentoring a young man named Anthony; and that he led a renovation project converting a Hardee's restaurant into a Christian-based teen activity center.

Bill's awakening challenge arrived in the spring of last year. He says, "When I learned there was an opening for the executive director of the Pulaski County Habitat for Humanity, I felt an unmistakable tugging of God in my heart to pursue it. It struck me as the perfect convergence of my passion for the poor and the skills and abilities that God has given to me."

Bill Promoting Habitat for Humanity

Guess what? Today Bill is serving in this capacity to provide decent housing to qualified low-income families. He feels that God is leveraging first-half learnings for eternal significance in his second half.

Acts chapter 7 concludes by reminding us that once Moses was willing to focus his life's energies in obedience to God's calling, he became an unstoppable force. This is most clearly seen when he is empowered by God to part the Red Sea and save his people.

Stage Four: Reaching Potential

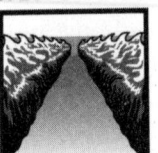

This fourth stage of the Halftime phenomenon is called "Reaching Potential." This last leg of a Halftimer's journey is about getting fully engaged in what he or she has been called to do in the second half. It involves seeking the right balance in serving, mixed with career responsibilities, family relationships, friendships, and recreational pursuits. Most importantly, it is about knowing that you are growing closer to God while partnering with him to do what he has designed and prepared for you to do. "For we are His workmanship, created in Christ Jesus for good works, which God prepared beforehand so that we would walk in them" (Eph. 2:10).

Foundation of Success, Journey Inward, Awakening Challenge, and Reaching Potential—these are the stages of the Halftime journey. Understanding each one is the first step toward partnering with a Halftimer on a great adventure.

THE SHARED MINISTRY MODEL

In a conference to five thousand pastors, Bill Hybels, founder and senior pastor of Willow Creek Community Church, made the following observations about the Halftime phenomenon.

> I'm operating with a theory these days that the greatest untapped resource in the next ten or fifteen years around the church is going to be all the people who are finishing life one—who don't want to just go to dinner at 5:30 and play shuffleboard. They love God, and they love our church. But we have to engage them at a whole different level than they could be engaged in life one when they were working sixty hours a week and commuting downtown. We have to tap into the incredible potential of all the life two, second-half people who are ready to give time, energy, resources, and experiences. They're ready to give it if we call them to it. If we don't call them to it, the call to golf might win.

Bill's right. We need to begin identifying these seasoned leaders and offer to help them direct a portion of their time, talent, and treasure toward greater meaning and a lasting legacy.

Don and Emily Renberg at First United Methodist Church in Tulsa illustrate the point. They are well known in a high-poverty neighborhood because of their ministry at the Eugene Field Elementary School. They visit often, sometimes for the entire day.

You see, the Renbergs coordinate an extensive mentoring program for students there.

They are not paid to do this. They want to do this. With their business savvy and entrepreneurial smarts, they have figured out how to genuinely help the Eugene Field community and how to recruit peers at church to lend a hand and heart at the school. They choose to invest their time, talent, and treasure in partnership with their church.

"Our pastors see the benefit in freeing leaders to do what God is calling them to do, and then they empower us to do it," says Clark Millspaugh, another volunteer at Eugene Field. Clark's day job involves running an oil and gas exploration company, but his passion is running the men's ministry at his church and involving others like himself.

First United Methodist is growing in influence for Christ by identifying and deploying Halftimers to do what God is calling them to do. The leadership has chosen a shared approach to accomplishing the work of the ministry (Eph. 4:11–12). It's a partnership!

Senior pastor Dr. Wade Paschal says, "We have a history of saying to people, 'Where do you think God wants this church to be in ministry?' and then giving them a real opportunity to do something about it."[14]

However, when Lloyd and I recently interviewed one hundred pastors from across the country who were thrilled with the prospects of seeing more people involved in ministry, they voiced some concerns. When asked what they perceived as the greatest barriers to cultivating a Halftime partnership in the church, two issues surfaced repeatedly: a fear of losing control and the challenge of overcoming existing church structures that would prevent this kind of entrepreneurship for God.

Serving on a large staff team for nearly thirty years in a church where close to six thousand people attend worship every Sunday, I have had to wrestle with these concerns myself. Our organizational

structure is fairly complex, representing multiple areas of ministry with all the accompanying volunteer needs.

I have learned that we need to offer two kinds of ministry partnerships through our churches: *limited partnerships* and *unlimited partnerships*. Both are essential.

Recently, a Halftimer approached Lloyd following a meeting with business leaders and pastors. He said, "I would love to be able to use my leadership skills in a leveraged way in my church, or through my church in our community, but sometimes I feel like a *limited partner*."

In business terms, a *limited partner* puts in his share of money, assumes minimal risk, and never really gets the opportunity to lead. Someone else is in charge.

In the church, *limited partnerships* are characterized by a member being asked to serve alongside a pastor or staff member to address a particular need inside the church. These opportunities for service include roles like Sunday school teacher, usher, choir member, small group leader, a children's or student worker, committee member, and so on. They are absolutely essential to the ongoing spiritual health of the church family.

However, the seasoned leaders that Lloyd and I are talking about are passionate to invest even more of their time, talent, and treasure to have an impact for God. They want an *unlimited partnership* that allows for fresh innovation. They need us to come alongside them to pursue a ministry inside or outside the church that aligns with their unique gifts, abilities, and passions. They want to be encouraged and empowered to lead a strategic ministry that advances the kingdom of God. (View an example of an Unlimited Partnership at www.SuccessToSignificance.com.)

My point is, you don't need to fear losing control of everything or feeling like you need to reorganize your entire church! Simply start with one *unlimited partnership* with a Halftimer and experience what the Lord can do.

Jesus' Ministry Model

I am inviting you to do what Jesus did. Let's take a moment to consider the pattern of leadership he modeled for us to imitate. Didn't he mobilize Halftimers like Peter; his brother Andrew; James, the son of Zebedee; John; Philip; Bartholomew; Thomas; Matthew; James, the son of Alphaeus; Thaddaeus; Simon, the zealot; and Judas Iscariot? His recruits were all adults who had achieved various levels of success and competence in the marketplace, from fishing to tax collection. These original Halftimers, save Judas, eventually left their first-half professions altogether to become leaders in the church—full-time pastors!

In a second wave of recruiting, our Lord added the apostle Paul. While he certainly invested the greatest percentage of his time in evangelism and church planting, we know that he continued to provide some of his financial support through his first-half occupation of making tents—part-time staff!

Jesus' leadership is the perfect model of shared ministry. He placed people in ministry positions according to their God-given gifts and abilities. He identified Halftimers, went to them on their turf, challenged them to join him, and unleashed them to do what God had created them to do. The partnership that he modeled changed the course of the world.

Paul offers these timeless principles about shared ministry in the first letter to the church at Corinth: "What, after all, is Apollos? And what is Paul? Only servants, through whom you came to believe—as the Lord has assigned each his task. I planted the seed, Apollos watered it, but God made it grow. So neither he who plants nor he who waters is anything, but only God, who makes things grow. The man who plants and the man who waters have one purpose, and each will be rewarded according to his own labor. For we are God's fellow workers; you are God's field, God's building" (1 Cor. 3:5–9 NIV).

Notice six clear principles reinforcing the pattern of shared ministry modeled by Jesus:

1. We all are Christ's servants and serve Christ as we serve others.
2. The Lord assigns tasks to each of us.
3. Our personal assignments are diverse in their contribution, but each contributes to the overall purpose of God.
4. All fruitful growth and ministry impact rests on the activity of God.
5. God rewards his laborers, and the reward is measured according to the individual's carrying out the assignment given.
6. We are in a dynamic partnership with God. He always initiates, and we are always responding to his lead.

This level of shared ministry between pastor and Halftimer may represent a new paradigm for some. It is a more decentralized model of ministry that empowers people to pursue their passions more freely in the context of their local church. It's a church like First United Methodist in Tulsa, OK; Willow Creek in Barrington, IL; Fellowship Bible Church in Little Rock, AR; Memorial Drive Presbyterian Church in Houston, TX; Mariners in Newport Beach, CA; Mecklenburg Community in Charlotte, NC; Saddleback in Lake Forest, CA; and others that are making programs and structures take second place to fresh vision that is unleashing Halftimers in unlimited ways. Yes, it is challenging to be more flexible, but the spiritual outcomes are beyond belief!

Barry, an orthopedic surgeon in Little Rock, and his wife Lynda are Halftimers. They lead a community-focused Common Cause group in partnership with their church. What the Lord has accomplished in and through their lives is truly amazing.

"During the first half of my medical career, I made my work my God," Barry confesses. "I thought I was getting satisfaction from that, but as a result of working too much and making extremely bad choices, my first marriage failed."

Three years later, Barry married Lynda, his present wife. The couple was "off in a similar direction" until they became captivated by the witness of another married couple. "Their marriage had something we wanted in ours. We became friends, and they invited us to attend Fellowship Bible Church in Little Rock. On November 22, 1985, Lynda and I prayed to receive Christ personally in the same church service."

Everything began changing for the two of them: the way they lived, the way they loved, and especially the way Barry interacted with his patients. "For the next twenty years I approached practicing medicine with a different attitude and a greater compassion. I began treating people rather than just diseases. I was open about my spirituality and prayed with my patients."

Barry accepted my invitation to be in my inaugural Kingdom Builders small group. In fact, this was the same Halftime-focused group I mentioned in chapter 1 in which Tom also participated. We spent many hours discussing his journey, his unique skills and abilities, and how the Lord might want to use him. I will never forget the morning that Barry shared his work story with our group. This was a project each participant completed so we could learn about one another's unique abilities and passions. Tears welled up in our eyes as they did in Barry's when he explained that he had never been given the opportunity to tell his story before. He felt loved and valued by us in a special way that morning. The lives of our small group of Halftimers were bonding, a bond that continues to this day. Barry was very uncertain about his future, but during our year together, God captured his heart with a ministry adventure that ideally fit his first-half learnings and personal passions.

"I knew I wanted to invest myself in the lives of those young men and women embarking on the same career path as my own. Historically, doctors are the world's worst at business. They graduate from medical school well trained in medicine but receive little in the way of education about investments, finance, real estate, family life, and other life skills."

With the support of Lynda, his Common Cause group, and church leaders, Barry approached the faculty at the University of Arkansas for Medical Sciences and asked if he could develop a program where community volunteers would teach the medical students life skills in nonmedical subjects. The faculty liked the idea, and soon the program that began as only a few days of elective lectures grew into a full week of lectures, called "The Life Skills Institute," which is now required for graduation from UAMS.

Barry Leading UAMS Life Skills Institute

"A lot of mentoring opportunities develop from these classes. There are no commercials, but we make it clear that the students are free to call any of these volunteers at any time. We don't go into the Institute with a religious agenda, but my prayer is that these students will see something unique about these leaders, and that is their personal relationship with Jesus Christ."

Barry will tell you that spearheading the Life Skills Institute has generated as much passion for him as his medical career. This wonderful outreach for Christ would never have occurred without a shared ministry model—a unique partnership between Halftimer and church pastor.

By the way, I had lunch with Barry recently. Working closely with our church's Community Strategies pastor, Barry is develop-

ing a new Life Skills Institute for inner city families and helping to launch a free medical clinic. It's almost beyond belief what God can accomplish when church leaders begin to partner with high-capacity Halftime leaders like Barry to pursue a calling of God.

In 2003, I was invited by Leadership Network (www.leadnet .org) to participate in a Leadership Community composed of leaders from twelve churches across the country. In fact, this is when my Halftime working relationship with Lloyd began. We convened four times over the next two years in three-day workshops to address the subject of how we could best connect with Halftimers in our churches and begin partnering with them in ministry.

The following diagram represents the "Shared Ministry Model" developed by our Leadership Community. It communicates a simple process to equip pastors to help Halftimers invest their time, talents, and treasure for eternal significance in the second half of life.

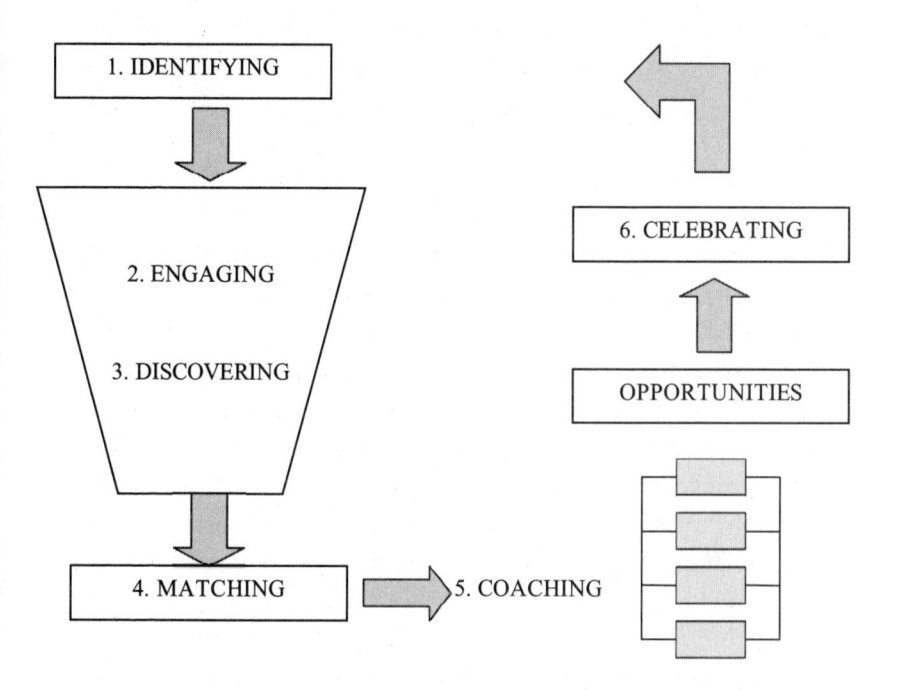

The Shared Ministry Model

This six-step diagram, which we call the Halftime Funnel, provides you with a clear relational process for developing your first partnership, with hopefully many others to follow. Here is a brief description of each step. I will unpack these in greater detail in the chapters that follow.

- *Identifying*—refers to a variety of practical ways to identify Halftimers in your church. I will share these with you at the conclusion of this chapter.
- *Engaging*—describes how to go about engaging Halftimers personally. A practical approach for establishing rapport and discussing the Halftime phenomenon at your first appointment will be presented.
- *Discovering*—provides you with proven assessment tools, Halftime learning experiences to explore, and other helpful Halftime resources for you to aid a Halftimer in discovering their God-given design, core strengths, and abilities.
- *Matching*—prepares you to interact with a Halftimer to match their design discovery to their best-fit opportunities for second-half service. For this discussion the Halftimer will complete a personal profile assignment on Lloyd's side of this flip-book. You also will be provided with a series of clarifying questions to ask and a catalog of ministry ideas and real-life examples to stimulate your partner's mind and heart regarding the "good work" the Lord has prepared for them to do.
- *Coaching*—addresses and helps you anticipate some of the needs and issues that a Halftimer experiences as they transition from the marketplace to the nonprofit world.
- *Celebrating*—shares some practical ideas to evaluate and celebrate what God accomplishes through your partnership. It also explains the power of using real-life stories to cast a broader vision to your church and community.

There you have it—the Halftime Funnel. It's your road map to starting your shared ministry model at your church, one partnership at a time.

Identifying Halftimers

This exciting journey begins by **Identifying** Halftimers in your church. How does a pastor go about doing this? I have personally utilized all five of the following approaches. The good news is, they work!

#1: The Season of Life Approach

Remember the MetLife research presented in chapter 1? For the most part, these people are baby boomers born between 1946 and 1964. Those experiencing Halftime are around fifty years old, plus or minus a few years either way, with thirty bonus years that no previous generation has ever had. This approach is very simple. Identify those in your church in this age group or season of life. Are they already involved in an area of ministry in your church? Get to know them. Do they have options about their future pace of work and available time? Perhaps one of these folks is interested in launching a part-time, parallel career in kingdom work.

#2: The Referral Approach

This is when someone you know well and trust refers a person experiencing the Halftime phenomenon to you. My good friend Tad, a small group leader in our church, told me that Mickey and his wife Phillis were members of his small group. Through his personal conversations with Mickey, Tad had learned Mickey was wondering how God might want him to invest his time, talent, and treasure in the future.

I contacted Mickey and began following the steps of the Shared Ministry Model. He was very excited about partnering with me. In the months that followed, we formed a great friendship around reading books related to his journey, helping him discover his

God-given design, praying for God to direct his path, and simply doing life together.

Recently, we celebrated God confirming Mickey's niche in ministry. He is starting a small group mentoring ministry, along with two friends, to help young entrepreneurial business leaders balance issues at work with their family responsibilities and church ministry involvement more effectively. Not a bad referral, wouldn't you agree?

#3: The Listening Approach

This may sound strange, but this is my number one approach to identifying Halftimers. It is a bit more intuitive in nature than the others. The listening approach means your Halftime antennae are operating all the time. You are listening in daily conversations to hear statements like: "I've just got this inner itch to do something, but I'm not sure what it is," or "I want to do something more meaningful or significant with my life." Others talk about leveraging first-half learnings and experiences in something new. Still others mention retirement and wonder how they will refocus their lives.

Remember Bill in chapter 2? I met Bill for the first time in my driveway when Carolyn and I were packing boxes to move our household. He mentioned to me that day that he was "sort of retired." My Halftime antennae sensed that he might be in Halftime. This led to our follow-up lunch appointment and partnership through the Halftime Funnel process. As previously stated, today Bill is executive director for Habitat for Humanity in central Arkansas.

#4: The Proven Track Record Approach

This technique for identifying Halftimers rests upon recognizing those in this season of life who have served in your church for years, perhaps in a variety of capacities. They have demonstrated spiritual maturity, leadership strength, and faithfulness. Their gifts, abilities, and passions are obvious to you because their proven track record has shown you what God created them to do.

In chapter 2, I introduced you to Linda through a series of questions she was asking herself while experiencing the journey inward stage of Halftime. Now it's time for the rest of her story.

Linda says, "Then came one of those rare 'aha' moments. I was sitting on the floor of my living room, going through old files, when I came upon a folder of my teaching notes that I had used when speaking to women's groups. As I sat there reviewing my talks, I found myself smiling at every illustration and reliving every moment. Before I knew it, several hours had passed. I'd been lost in my passion—ministering to women and using my gifts. Why had it taken me so long to 'get it'—to understand what I had been created by God to do?

"Soon thereafter I quit my job. For the last six years, I have been doing what energizes me the most, ministering to women in my church and working with women one-on-one as a certified Life Coach. I'm busier than ever and loving every minute of it!"

Linda, her husband Dave, and their children have been members of our church for twenty years. Repeatedly, Linda has proven herself faithful by serving in a variety of capacities. Now, she has found her niche.

Linda with Halftimers

My knowledge of her proven track record at Fellowship is what led me to challenge her to partner with me on a part-time basis to direct our Halftime ministry to women. I knew she would be a great fit because I had witnessed her in action for years. Linda has already written a workbook called *Woman on a Mission*. Using this material, she is teaching an evening class and a morning class every week to help other women discover their purpose and mission in life like she has.

She continues one-on-one life coaching and is thrilled that other churches are beginning to order her *Woman on a Mission* workbook for their ministry to women.

"Gone is the sick feeling that I was wasting the one life I had been given. I have found great joy and deep meaning because I know that my contribution glorifies God. I am doing what he created me to do."

#5: The Cold Call Approach

This doesn't mean that you are making a "cold call," but that you are *receiving* one from a Halftimer who has questions.

Kris was not a member of Fellowship when he called me. I had never met him before. Kris had participated in a Men's Fraternity class of one thousand men that Robert Lewis and I had taught called "The Great Adventure." This course addresses how God has uniquely wired every person and the legacy he desires for us to pursue.

A week or so after the class, Kris called to say he had attended our sessions and had some questions he would like to discuss. He asked me if I would meet him for lunch at a local restaurant to do so. I said yes, and I am forever thankful that I did.

At lunch, I discovered that Kris was a very gifted plastic surgeon who was experiencing a Halftime journey. He shared his life story with me, his passion for the people of Honduras, and his confusion about what God wanted him to do.

Inside my heart, I sensed the Lord telling me to invite Kris to join my Halftimers small group for the upcoming year. I told him about it, and he agreed to rearrange his surgical schedule on the spot in order to participate.

During that year, we forged a remarkable friendship as we made our way through the steps of the Shared Ministry Model. We brainstormed numerous ministry strategies to discover the approach that best utilized his time, talent, and treasure. And God showed Kris what he wanted him to do.

Kris now takes surgical teams to Honduras several times a year to repair physical deformities in children and adults that most Honduran doctors aren't equipped to restore. God has used him to establish a special relationship with the founder of a privately-owned hospital who is making the surgical suite available to Kris's team at no charge. More recently, God has begun opening new doors of opportunity for Kris and his team of doctors, nurses, and hospital administrators to connect with Honduran doctors in a medical school to teach them surgical skills to heal their people.

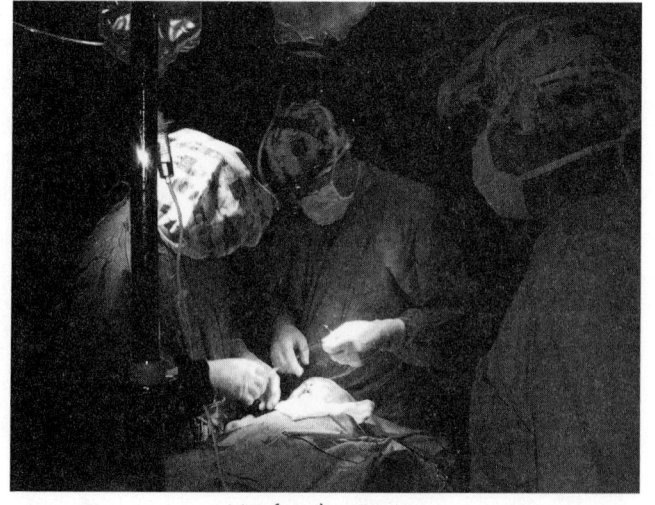

Kris (center) in Honduras

Kris and his family have joined our church and are growing spiritually through one of our small groups, and I marvel at all that God is doing in and through his life. It's the best cold call I have ever received!

All five of these approaches to identifying Halftimers in your church really work. Give them a try. You'll be glad you did!

CHAPTER 4

INVESTING IN A HALFTIMER

A number of years ago, I taught a sermon from the second chapter of Paul's first letter to the church at Thessalonica. It is a familiar passage where the apostle uses three different metaphors to communicate the importance of investing in others: the faithful steward, the nursing mother, and the mentoring father.

I defined investing as "having a passionate desire to be used by God to help someone else grow spiritually." It's when you equip another person to walk in the truth or to discover their one-of-a-kind design from God or to help an individual find their place of service for the Lord.

Perhaps a few biblical examples will help illustrate the point. Investing is what Jethro did for Moses when he taught his son-in-law the invaluable lesson on delegation. It is what Moses did for Joshua when he prepared his faithful lieutenant to lead Israel into the promised land. Investing is what Paul did for Timothy when he invited him to go on a missionary journey that later enabled him to pastor a dynamic church in Ephesus. An opportunity with the potential for a great return on investment is what the Lord has arranged for you and me as pastors through the Halftime phenomenon.

Pastors across the continent consistently describe a leadership gap between their need for qualified leaders to help expand the ministry of the church and the number of church staff members

they can afford to hire. I believe that investing in Halftimers represents an unprecedented opportunity to fill this gap.

Mike's story at the beginning of chapter 2 is a perfect example.
Our church was growing in number, and my responsibilities were
increasing simultaneously. We needed more children's space, so
our elders determined to move our staff from the office space we
occupied on campus near our worship center and renovate it to
better accommodate the needs of our younger families. This led to
the construction of a new facility across the street for staff offices
and some multipurpose meeting rooms for ministry. The idea of
adding this new building project to my already packed personal
schedule felt overwhelming.

Mike (center) at church construction site

Mike's God-given skills and abilities were a perfect fit. We met
together on a regular basis to discuss the progress of the project
and to solve on-site challenges that occur in any construction job.
But Mike's daily oversight saved me hundreds of hours of meetings
with contractors, architects, and engineers. In fact, he completed
this project on time, within our budget guidelines, and with excellence. God used a seasoned leader and great partner to fill a sig-

nificant leadership gap for our church. He gave us his time, and we gave him a cell phone and computer to do his work. That's what I call an unbelievable return on investment!

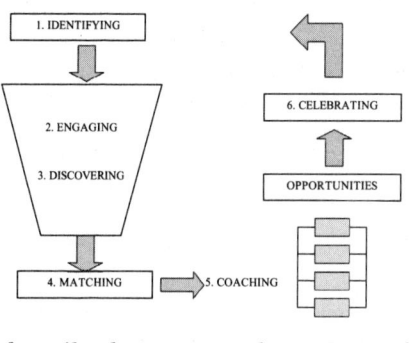

In the last chapter, I introduced the Shared Ministry Model (left) and explained five proven approaches for **Identifying** (Step 1) Halftimers in your church. Now, I want to take you into the heart of the Halftimer Funnel to describe how to go about **Engaging** (Step 2) a Halftimer that you have identified and how to help them **Discover** (Step 3) their **Core** or their God-given strengths, abilities, and passions.

By investing in this manner, God will use you to facilitate the Halftimer's journey inward toward greater self-understanding. Here is some practical advice for establishing rapport and discussing the Halftime phenomenon at your first meeting together.

Business Leader Profile

There are a few things you need to know about most high-capacity leaders before your initial appointment.

- They work long hours in a fast-paced, highly competitive environment. No one gives them permission to get off the marketplace treadmill to reflect and consider their future contribution for God to others.
- They are more familiar with how to get things done in the marketplace than in the nonprofit world and are somewhat uncertain how to bridge that gap.
- When a pastor contacts them, the most frequent perception is that they are being approached to meet a financial need in the church or fill a ministry need that may or may not fit their unique design from God.

- Some even feel that God can't use their leadership savvy, first-half learnings, and marketplace business skills in the ministry world because this has not been envisioned for them in a challenging and exciting manner.
- Few have had a pastor pursue them on their turf with the idea of partnering together, focusing on helping the Halftimer discover their design and personal calling from God.

Before going any further, there is one point of clarification that I want to make about investing in your Halftime partner. While I have had many appointments with women in Halftime to discuss their assessment results, brainstorm ministry ideas, and help them find their fit in serving the Lord, the heart or more personal aspect of this journey should be processed with a spiritually mature woman. I recommend that church leaders identify a female counterpart, possibly your women's ministry leader, to help facilitate this phase of the Halftime journey. This is what Linda (chap. 2) does for me with such wisdom and understanding. If there is not a woman in your church who you feel can play this role, then point your female Halftimer to a woman in your community that is known as a spiritual leader.

Beyond this, encourage her to visit www.SuccessToSignificance .com to view the personal testimonies of women who have worked through this issue themselves. There is also a list of Halftime coaches for women to contact on this Web site.

Be Proactive

Schedule an appointment to begin building your relationship. I have met Halftimers at my office, their office, for coffee, and over lunch. My favorite is over lunch because sharing a meal together in a nice environment facilitates friendly conversation. It's a little thing, but I like to pay for their lunch.

From previous appointments like this, I have discovered a repetition of the topics that are most frequently discussed. Interestingly, they flow neatly from the acrostic FORMAT. Please notice that ask-

ing questions and listening for answers, with your Halftime antennae up, are the two most important skills you need at lunch. This is
my suggested FORMAT for your first meeting:

F—Family: Begin by asking your Halftimer to tell you about
their *family* background, marriage, children, and so forth. You
could share yours as well.

O—Occupation: Ask them to tell you about their *occupational*
history, including vocational changes, jobs they have really enjoyed,
and roles they have played in each. You likely will hear some information at this point that will give you some idea about their unique
gifting and what energizes them.

R—Relationship with God/Religious Background: Inquire
about their *relationship* with God or their *religious* background.
Listen to hear if they are a new Christian, a growing Christ-
follower, or if there are some spiritual needs that you could speak
to or offer to pray about with them.

M—Ministry: What *ministry* experience have they had in the
past? Was it a position in the church, a service project in the community, or serving on a mission team in another country? How did
they contribute? What role did they play? What skills did they
use? What did they enjoy doing the most from their ministry experiences? Again, listen carefully for their design capabilities and for
areas of passion.

A—Ask: Ask them if they are familiar with the Halftime phenomenon. If they are, request that they share their learnings with
you and how they believe these experiences apply to their life.

T—Tell: Finally, *tell* them what you have been learning about
Halftime in the church and the exciting possibilities it offers. The
first three chapters of this book provide you with plenty of information to do this. You could use your book to highlight some of the
aspects that were most important to you. For example, sharing and
discussing the identifiable stages of Halftime from the life of Moses
presented in chapter 2 may provide you with a great opportunity to
define the stage your Halftimer is experiencing.

Also tell them of your interest in exploring a Halftime partnership. Explain that the next step is simply to read this book forward and backward and schedule a follow-up appointment (about two weeks out) to further discuss Halftime in more detail based upon your reading.

The FORMAT is that simple. This first lunch appointment is about asking questions and listening very carefully to the answers. It's about gauging where your Halftimer is in their journey and their level of interest in pursuing a partnership with you.

Bob Buford enjoyed the investment of Peter Drucker in his life for many years. He writes that they were talking on one occasion about what Bob might do for others. Bob says, "When Peter gave me his answer, I realized that it was what he had done for me as well."

Peter said, "You can't invent community leaders, but you may be able to identify them, equip them, and give them what they need very badly—somebody to hold their hands. I am busier than I have ever been as a consultant, but, primarily, the people who come to me do so because nobody else listens to them. Not that I can always help them, but I'm willing to listen, and I'm able to say, 'Look, Joe, this is a molehill. Don't make a mountain out of it.' Or, 'Listen, Joe, you are creating a democracy; you are not creating leadership.' My function is not to tell them. My function is to get them to hear themselves talk and to listen to themselves."

This is a wonderful description of how to **Engage** (Step 2) a Halftimer over lunch and begin to build a relationship.

You are now halfway through the Halftime Funnel (right), your roadmap to starting a Shared Ministry Model at your church, one partnership at a time. A follow-up appointment has been scheduled to discuss insights about Halftime from

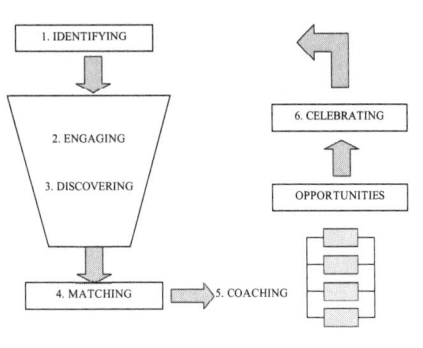

two vantage points: (1) the Halftimer and (2) the pastor. Both parties are reading and reviewing both sides of this book to prepare for their next interaction.

Invariably, in your follow-up appointment, a series of questions will surface that are related to how the Halftimer will go about **Discovering** (Step 3) their core or God-given design strengths, abilities, and passions. Questions like: What can I do to better understand how God has wired me? What am I good at doing? What energizes me? And how does the Lord want me to serve others?

Author Stephen Covey writes about this discovery process in his best-selling book *The 8th Habit.* He encourages leaders to find their "voice" or unique design, and inspire others to do the same. He encourages people to maximize their strengths. This discovery process is initiated in Step 3 of the Halftime Funnel.

Three Foundational Concepts

Before I recommend two excellent assessment tools for making design discoveries, I want to equip you with three foundational biblical concepts that will serve you well in providing your Halftimers with a vision of the Creator's handiwork in their lives.

1. The first foundational concept is that God is the *Creator of giftedness.* Giftedness refers to your one-of-a-kind design from God. It includes a combination of God-given talents and abilities received at conception and spiritual gifts received at conversion. These should be viewed as complementary and not in opposition to each other. In most instances, spiritual gifts energize, enrich, and empower God's original design. Conversion changes the useful purpose of your original design but not God's creative handiwork.

Reflect upon David's words with **conception** in mind. "For You formed my inward parts; You wove me in my mother's womb. I will give thanks to You, for I am fearfully and wonderfully made; wonderful are Your works, and my soul knows it very well. My frame was not hidden from You, when I was made in secret, and

skillfully wrought in the depths of the earth; Your eyes have seen my unformed substance; and in Your book were all written the days that were ordained for me, when as yet there was not one of them" (Ps. 139:13–16).

Consider the apostle Paul's words with **conversion** in mind: "Since we have gifts that differ according to the grace given to us, each of us is to exercise them accordingly" (Rom. 12:6).

You and I are "fearfully and wonderfully" crafted by God. We have been given spiritual "gifts that differ," making each person a unique and special creation of his. Giftedness is from God and reminds us that we are one of a kind.

2. The second foundational concept is that God is the *Author of personal calling.* Calling refers to God's invitation to you and me to partner with him to do the "good works" he has prepared for you and me, according to our giftedness.

Paul writes in his letter to the church at Ephesus, "For we are His workmanship, created in Christ Jesus for good works, which God prepared beforehand, that we should walk in them" (Eph. 2:10).

Don't miss the connection between his gifting and his calling in our personal lives. Paul is saying that God has hot-wired you and me with great intentionality; we are "His workmanship." He wants us to join him in accomplishing good works that he has "prepared beforehand" for us to do. This is our calling. Therefore, a great indicator to help Halftimers discover their calling is to confirm their giftedness. God does not form and equip our lives with precise intention only to call you or me to do something that does not fit who we are.

3. The third foundational concept is that God is the *Originator of purpose.* While our gifting is one of a kind, and our calling represents certain works he has authored in advance for us to discover and accomplish, there is a universal purpose that all Christ-followers are to pursue: to glorify God above all else, forever.

Listen to these words of Peter: "As each one has received a

special gift, employ it in serving one another, as good stewards of the manifold grace of God. Whoever speaks, let him speak, as it were, the utterances of God; whoever serves, let him do so as by the strength which God supplies: so that in all things God may be glorified through Jesus Christ, to whom belongs the glory and dominion forever and ever. Amen" (1 Pet. 4:10–11).

I have shared these biblical concepts on numerous occasions with a Halftimer to set the stage for the process of **Discovering** (Step 3) more about their core strengths and abilities as a preparation to **Matching** (Step 4) the design discoveries with ministry opportunities, or callings, that fit their unique design.

Two Assessment Tools

Now, let's turn our attention to the two recommended assessment tools that I mentioned earlier. Both are online inventories that provide a printed profile of the user's answers. Both are well researched and tested. Both represent easy-to-understand tools for making personal design discoveries. However, neither should be viewed as the "voice of God" in the matter, but rather as a practical tool revealing insights into a person's strengths and abilities that can be discussed, confirmed by others, prayed about, and utilized to help a Halftimer understand more about what God has created them to do. Keep in mind that Halftime is a process or journey, not simply a test result.

The StrengthsFinder® Profile: To take advantage of this inventory, purchase the book *Living Your Strengths* (by Albert L. Winseman, Donald O. Clifton, and Curt Liesveld). You will find a code on the inside of the book cover that enables you to go online at www.strengthsfinder.com to complete your assessment.

The Servants by Design™ Inventory: To take advantage of this inventory, go online to www.youruniquedesign.com and complete your assessment. This is the inventory we use at Fellowship Bible Church in Little Rock. It has helped thousands of people learn more about their God-given design.

Your Halftimer will become familiar with these two assessment options from their reading. They may have already completed one or both of them. If this is the case and they have their personal profile results with them, ask them to share their design discoveries with you. Specifically ask them to point out the discoveries they believe represent the most accurate picture of who they really are.

Whether they have their inventory results handy or not, give the following Halftime homework assignment for your next visit. You should make a copy of this assignment from the pages of your book in advance to be given to your partner at this time.

Halftime Homework Assignment

The marketplace leader should answer the following three questions and make a first pass at writing a single-paragraph design description of the real you.

What are my greatest strengths according to the inventory that I completed? _____

_____

_____

_____

_____

What skills and abilities were identified that represent the ones I enjoy using the most? _____

_____

_____

_____

_____

From my reading of Halftime stories, my discussions with others, and my inventory results, have there been any subject matters, compelling causes, groups of people, or passions tugging on my heartstrings? If so, list them here:

_____

_____

_____

_____

Here is a sample design description you can follow in taking a first pass at writing your own:

> *God has uniquely designed me to "use my organizational skills and my relational abilities to accomplish significant tasks or projects and to bring practical wisdom and encouragement to others."*

Now, you give it a try. Your design description does not have to be perfect. Your goal is to begin to capture the essence of your **Core,** the Creator's handiwork in your life. Pray about this as you write. God will guide you.

First Pass Design Description

God has uniquely designed me to . . . .

_____

_____

_____

_____

_____

_____

_____

This subject of understanding the core of your design is explored more deeply in Lloyd Reeb's book *From Success to Significance.* It is available, together with small group curriculum, at www.SuccessToSignificance.com.

One Thing

Years ago, my wife Carolyn and I were on vacation in Colorado Springs. One evening we went to see the movie *City Slickers*. At one point in the film, Jack Palance and Billy Crystal are riding along on their horses, having a conversation about life and what every person needs to know. It went like this:

Palance: "Do you know what the secret of life is?"

Crystal: "No, what?"

Palance: "This." (holding out his index finger)

Crystal: "Your finger?"

Palance: "One thing, just one thing."

Crystal: "That's great, but what's the one thing?"

Palance: "That's what you've got to figure out."

I believe that the "one thing" is understanding our unique God-given design, our giftedness, and helping Halftimers do the same. It's helping them find their "voice."

When Kevin finished law school, he joined one of the larger law firms in Little Rock. He has enjoyed a successful first-half practice as a merger/acquisitions and securities attorney.

He began his Halftime journey in his early thirties when he began to question what he wanted to do with the rest of his life. Married and the father of two children, he was wondering how all this was going to work. He was convinced that God had something more for him, but he didn't know what it was or how to get there.

My first appointment with Kevin was over some delicious ice cream late one afternoon. He had completed the "Servants by Design™ Inventory" and brought his profile results along. We had a great time highlighting the *Core* of his design. I asked him if he would like to partner with me and a few other Halftimers to explore his journey further, and he agreed.

During the course of our time together, in a small group context, I assigned the design description project. I even challenged

each Halftimer to come up with a single word, the "one thing" that captured how God had uniquely made them.

Kevin says, "A few nights before I presented my design description to the group, I sat in bed and discussed with my wife who God created me to be. We had been processing my journey together all along the way. I had a few personal characteristics that I was sharing with Elicia when she stopped me and said, 'You are a guide to others, Kevin.' I thought about the word *guide* for a few moments. My heart began to stir with excitement. She was right; God created me to be a 'guide.'"

You cannot imagine how freeing this discovery has been to Kevin and how much confidence it has given him regarding the "good works" God created him to do. Kevin is not only using his God-given gifts and abilities to guide others in the marketplace, but he also has joined me in guiding Halftimers to discover their "one thing."

Once your Halftimer begins to have confidence about their **Core,** you can begin to explore other Halftime learning experiences together to build your relationship and to focus on **Capacity** (creating time availability to begin giving themselves away) and **Context** (the type of ministry, role, and environment that best fits their design).

How to go about doing this will be explained in the next chapter on **Matching** (Step 4) giftedness or design with personal calling. There is a connection between the two because our sovereign God is behind both, longing for a partnership with each of us.

CHAPTER 5

MATCHING GIFTEDNESS WITH PERSONAL CALLING

atching first-half-of-life learnings with second-half-of-life call-ings seemed to just fall into place for Linda. As this Halftimer puts it, "God revealed to me and my husband, Dean, that all of the pain we had suffered would not go to waste."

In the early 1980s, Linda found herself divorced and raising two young children alone. Having a career outside the home was no longer an option but a shocking necessity. At the core, God gifted her with exceptional administrative skills and the ability to relate well to people. She found her marketplace niche in an accounting firm utilizing these talents. She was hired as an office manager, and she enjoyed that position for six years.

During this time period, she met a wonderful Christian man at church. After dating for several years, Linda and Dean were married. Both were busy with careers and family responsibilities; but because both had been through the painful process of divorce and experienced the ramifications firsthand, God placed in their hearts a special calling for divorce prevention. The suffering they had experienced in the first half of life would not "go to waste."

Linda's Tapestry

Linda and Dean joined a cause-focused small group at Fellowship composed of previously divorced couples who also

had a heart for those contemplating the destruction of their marriages. They understood from their own experiences that others facing this situation needed a mentor. Group members knew these hurting couples needed someone who had lived through the nightmares of divorce to challenge them with God's perspectives on taking the course of action they were pursuing. Since coming together, Linda and this loving team of lay people have been used by God to save numerous marriages in crisis. But God was not through matching Linda's unique design strengths with special places of service.

Linda and Dean (second from left)

In the midst of mentoring couples in crisis, Linda read an ad in the church bulletin reporting the need for an executive-level staff assistant to work with two teaching pastors. The gifts and talents needed for this position were proven administrative abilities and people skills. God was about to make another match between Linda's *Core* (God-given strengths, abilities, and passions) and her *Context* (type of ministry, role, and working environment).

She says, "My heart began beating excitedly. I wondered if God was opening a new opportunity for me—from corporate world to church world. I finally felt his peace and his leading to apply for the

job." Of course, when she did, we snatched her up immediately. She was a perfect fit!

When I asked Linda recently about her journey, she responded,

> It is so gratifying to walk through the church lobby on Sunday morning and see a young couple we mentored when they were lost, hurting, and ready to call a divorce attorney, now holding hands on the way to a worship service. God has blessed me. He has placed me in a strategic position on staff to use the gifts and abilities he gave me to serve others administratively and to speak into the lives of broken relationships. My heart is filled with satisfaction and joy when I reflect upon God's handiwork in my life. He has woven a beautiful tapestry, turning my past sufferings and life experiences into things that are eternally significant. I am forever grateful.

So am I. Prior to my transition from teaching pastor to church planting and consulting, I had the privilege of partnering with Linda for five years. Let me just put it this way: our church is a better place because of her investment of time and talent.

However, matching a Halftimer's *Core* (strengths, abilities, and passions) with their *Capacity* (time availability for giving themselves away to others) and *Context* (type of ministry, role, and best-fit environment) does not always fall into place as naturally as it did for Linda.

Every Halftimer's matching process is unique. Some are crystal clear about their design discoveries, passions, and place of service; others find this challenging; still others experience **Matching** (Step 4) as the most difficult step in the Shared Ministry Model.

So, let's review for a moment and then tackle this challenge. We have moved through the first three steps of the Halftime Funnel (above right): Identifying, Engaging, and Discovering. Most recently, your Halftimer has completed an assessment tool, answered a few probing questions, taken a first pass at writing a per-

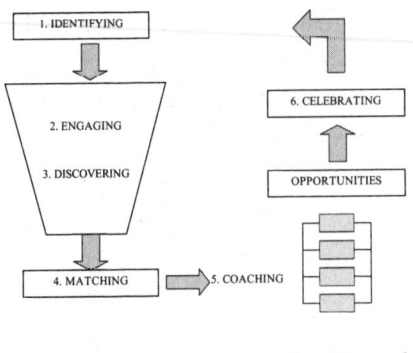

sonal design description, and interacted with you about all of these. There should be a growing confidence in your Halftime partner about their **Core** (God-given strengths and abilities).

The movement from inside the Funnel (**Discovering,** Step 3) to outside the Funnel (**Matching,** Step 4) turns our focus to the subject of implementation, or learning how to put the Halftimer's design discoveries to use in a manner that is a best-fit for them, that will bless others, and that glorifies Jesus Christ.

The apostle Peter writes, "As each one has received a special gift, employ it in serving one another as good stewards of the manifold grace of God. Whoever speaks, is to do so as one who is speaking the utterances of God; whoever serves is to do so as one who is serving by the strength which God supplies; so that in all things God may be glorified through Jesus Christ, to whom belongs the glory and dominion forever and ever. Amen" (1 Pet. 4:10–11).

Discovering (Step 3) accents the Head Journey referred to in chapter 2. **Matching** (Step 4) accents the Heart Journey. It is important that you encourage your Halftime partner to seek the heart of God about this decision. "'For I know the plans that I have for you,' declares the Lord, 'plans for welfare and not for calamity to give you a future and a hope. Then you will call upon Me and come and pray to Me, and I will listen to you. And you will seek Me and find Me, when you search for Me with all your heart'" (Jer. 29:11–13).

For a Halftimer to have confidence about matching their **Core** with their **Capacity** and their **Context,** they must know of God's involvement, just like Linda did. So what does a pastor do at this critical point in the Shared Ministry Model to assist a Halftimer in finding their ministry match?

I encourage you to choose one or more of the following pathways to help your Halftimer find their best-fit.

Pathways to Matching

Pathway #1: Go Exploring

This first pathway invites you to grow together in your understanding through either a hands-on learning experience, an educational learning experience, or an interactive learning experience. Let me explain each one.

Hands-On Learning Experience. Do an urban plunge, inner city work project (like building a Habitat for Humanity house), or go on a missions trip together. This offers several benefits: time to continue building your relationship, leadership development, processing time, and a totally different environment that the Lord will use to speak into the heart of your Halftimer.

Steve with Honduran girl

A decade ago, Steve, a physician at Arkansas Children's Hospital, went on his first medical/evangelism missions trip to Tegucigalpa, Honduras, where Fellowship has a ministry partnership with World Gospel Outreach. From this first hands-on learning experience, the Lord moved in Steve's heart, giving him an

overwhelming passion for the needs of the Honduran people. For the last ten years, he has led nearly every medical/evangelism team we have sent there. God has effectively used Steve's leadership to expose hundreds of our church members to the desperate needs of others in a third-world country, to utilize their gifts and abilities to care for them, and to learn how to trust their Heavenly Father for those outside their comfort zones.

Educational Learning Experience. Attend a nearby Success to Significance Summit or Significance Weekend. Visit www .SuccessToSignificance.com for up-to-date information and details. The benefit of this approach is the opportunity to connect with other pastors and Halftimers sharing your same journey. Led by a Halftime coach, your questions will be answered by an expert. You also will learn about other helpful Halftime resources.

I attended my first Halftime learning event (called a Success to Significance Summit) at a Methodist church where we spent the better part of a day working through a *Discovering Your Game Plan* notebook. Arriving early, I placed my briefcase and notebook at a table near the front, and then went to get some refreshments. As the meeting began, I was delighted to discover that Steve, a friend, church member, and business leader was seated at the same table. During the lunch break, Steve said, "This information is tremendous. It explains right where I am in my life, but I don't have a clue how God might want to use my gifts and abilities in the future."

I asked Steve a simple question about things he was passionate about. He responded, "What I am most passionate about right now is my company's involvement in the relief effort to aid victims of Hurricane Katrina. We are partnering with a church in Louisiana to help people."

Coincidentally, the very next day in an elders meeting, our board was discussing our church's role in the same relief effort. Someone mentioned that a disaster relief leadership team was being formed with the help of Ray, one of our community strategies pastors. I was asked if I knew a Halftimer who had the skills

and abilities to co-lead our church's response. Without hesitation, because of my previous conversations, I said, "As a matter of fact, I do," thinking of Steve. Steve was on board by the end of the day. Is God good at arranging the unexpected or what? This Summit was a very helpful learning experience for both of us.

Interactive Learning Experience. Benefit from an interactive learning experience if a Halftime event is not easily accessible to you. Work through the *Success to Significance* small group curriculum and DVD series together. As you know from my stories, I often include several Halftimers in this small group experience. Doing this together affords the opportunity to process heart and faith issues with your Halftimer that surround **Matching** (Step 4). This approach will introduce you to many stories of what other Halftimers are doing in their second half and how they partnered with their pastor. One segment explains the dynamics of this partnership and offers additional Halftime resources that also could be explored this way.

So, the first pathway is all about exploration—through a hands-on learning experience, an educational opportunity, or an interactive learning exposure.

Pathway #2: Gather the Existing

This second pathway encourages you to develop and keep an up-to-date list of high-capacity ministry roles that a Halftimer could fill if it **Matched** (Step 4) their design strengths and personal passions. These can be identified by thinking about service opportunities you likely already have in three different spheres of influence:

- *Church*: A leadership role inside your church.
- *Community*: A ministry opportunity outside your church, addressing a vital need in your city or town.
- *Country*: A missions-related position in another country where your church has an existing partnership.

This is a very important pathway for pastors to cultivate. Reflecting on the MetLife research in chapter 1, "Nearly half (48 per-

cent) of Americans age fifty to seventy think it may be difficult to find good work." I believe that churches should become the gate-keepers for connecting Halftimers to challenging, best-fit roles in one of these spheres of influence—church, community, and country. But these "good works" must be envisioned by pastors for those who are anxious to find their fit and to serve.

Over the past several years, numerous ministry opportunities for Halftimers have been on our radar screen. Time after time, God has raised up a leader whose *Core, Capacity,* and *Context* fit an existing need we had identified in one of these three arenas. I hope this list of a dozen of them will stimulate your thinking about possible serving options in your church, your community, or a country in which you have a mission partnership.

Ministry Opportunity and Sphere of Influence	
Ministry Opportunity	**Sphere of Influence**
Ministry to Single Parents—Offering free auto clinics, home repair, mentoring of children, and tons of compassion.	Church & Community
Missions Trip Coordinator—Leading teams of people on various mission projects.	Country
Life Skills Director—Overseeing qualified volunteer teams to teach inner city parents about child-rearing, budgeting, healthcare, employment, etc.	Community
Pre-Marriage Preparation/Mentoring—Leading pre-marital counseling and first-year-of-marriage mentoring in small groups.	Church
Executive Director for Habitat for Humanity—Providing decent housing and ministry to qualified low-income families.	Community

Men's Fraternity Administrator/Host — Overseeing a team of volunteers providing a ministry to more than 1,000 men (more than 50 percent are not members at Fellowship) on the subject of manhood. Serves as host and ministry partner with Pastor Robert Lewis, founder of the Men's Fraternity curriculum and video series (www.mensfraternity.com).	Church & Community
Campus/Facilities Director—Overseeing the care, maintenance, and upgrading of grounds and facility-related needs.	Church
Community Strategies Director — Researcher gathering information about the top needs of our community and the nonprofit organizations that are best addressing the needs. Identifies partnership possibilities and leadership opportunities.	Community
President and Chief Executive Officer of World Gospel Outreach — Leading this organization that ministers to homeless children in Tegucigalpa, Honduras.	Country
Director of Kingdom Building for Women — Leading a special aspect of our Women's Ministry to help women experiencing Halftime find their place of service in one of the three spheres of ministry opportunity.	Church & Community
Moms 'n More Mentor — Giving younger mothers (40 percent of which are not members at Fellowship) a spiritual perspective on the significant investment they are making in their marriage and children as described in Titus 2:3–4.	Church & Community
Disaster Relief Team Leader — Overseeing a volunteer response team to meet the needs of those facing a catastrophic circumstance due to fire, tornado, hurricane, flooding, etc.	Community & Country

The writer of Hebrews says, "Let us consider how to stimulate one another to love and good deeds" (Heb. 10:24). I hope that my list of a dozen Halftimer-led ministries does this for you. Develop your up-to-date list of high-capacity ministry roles that a Halftimer could fill if it matches their design strengths and personal passions and keep it in front of you. You will be amazed and thrilled by the partnerships that God puts together!

On Tuesday mornings at Fellowship, young moms meet in the parking lot to walk in together. They are hauling diaper bags, purses, strollers, infant carriers, babies, and toddlers. It takes great effort to get themselves and their offspring there, but they are motivated by the rich fellowship and encouragement they receive at Moms 'n More, a women's ministries class designed just for them.

It is in this *Context* (type of ministry, role, and working environment) that Bette found a match for her *Core* (God-given design, strengths, and abilities).

Married for forty-five years, the mother of two and grandmother of six, this Halftimer is a treasure chest of practical wisdom and encouragement for young mothers. But it was her first-half learnings and experiences as a guidance counselor for fourteen years in the public school system that God used to place this passion for parenting in Bette's heart.

She says, "My role as a mentor in Moms 'n More fits me so well. I became aware of the great needs of both children and parents as a guidance counselor. By the time I retired from my career, I knew God was calling me to work with young mothers at Fellowship."

That was ten years ago. Since then, Bette has personally mentored 150 women. Translate that into 150 families in which she has invested her life, and the ripple effect on the lives of husbands and children is infinite.

Camille, another Halftimer who is the Moms 'n More teaching leader at Fellowship, says, "Bette sets the standard for being an incredible mentor for every young woman that joins her group

Bette with Young Moms

each year. She is wonderful at presenting God's truth about marriage and motherhood with grace and encouragement."

Bette found her best-fit role in an existing ministry inside our church. Another Mike, on the other hand, found his match in an existing ministry in another country altogether.

Before becoming president and chief executive officer of World Gospel Outreach, a ministry to homeless children in Tegucigalpa, Honduras, Mike was a partner in a local construction company with another man in our church. They specialized in remodeling large homes, new residential projects, and limited commercial work. These partners experienced great fulfillment using their construction skills on a few missions trips with our church to Honduras.

Helping to build housing for street children at Rancho Ebenezer for World Gospel Outreach is what God used to speak to Mike's heart. "I had never even thought about missions work before," says Mike. "That's when I learned that World Gospel Outreach needed someone on-site in Honduras to coordinate all of their ministry operations. It was a good match for me. More importantly, I experienced an undeniable call of God in my heart

Mike and Lyn at Rancho Ebenezer

to pursue the position." Today, Mike is leading this wonderful ministry in Honduras with excellence.

The second pathway is about taking advantage of existing ministry opportunities in one of three spheres of influence—church, community, or country. It's about developing and keeping an up-to-date list of serving opportunities in each to help a Halftimer find their best-fit.

Pathway #3: Get Entrepreneurial

This third pathway offers an opportunity for **Matching** (Step 4) a Halftimer's unique design abilities with a calling that fits their giftedness through some out-of-the-box thinking about new ways to minister to the needs of others. That is, you or a Halftimer conceive a new endeavor that does not currently exist in your church, your community, or another country where you have a ministry partnership. I want to recommend three practical methods for benefiting from this final pathway for **Matching** (Step 4): form a dream team, find out from peers, or flex with your Halftimer's idea.

Form a Dream Team. Assemble a small group of strategic thinkers to brainstorm with your Halftime partner about possible

applications for their design strengths and abilities in areas of personal passion. Use the Halftimer's assessment tool results, design description, and other self-appraisal information to guide your think tank group, which could be made up of other staff members, marketplace leaders, or friends who are willing to act as a "dream team" or "personal board" on behalf of the Halftimer to help flesh out a best-fit serving role. You will be surprised at the level of idea generation that can take place in just a couple of hours! Keep in mind that matching is a process, and don't be concerned if an immediate discovery for serving is not identified.

Find Out from Peers. Encourage your Halftime partner to read stories in Bob Buford's book *Finishing Well* or online at www.SuccessToSignificance.com about what other Halftimers are doing to build God's kingdom. The Lord may use an entrepreneurial idea that they read about to capture their imagination and heart. Peer learning like this is an excellent method for discovering fresh ministry approaches.

Flex with Your Halftimer's Idea. Be open to help a Halftimer pursue their entrepreneurial ministry idea. This will not happen frequently, but when it does, it can be a thrilling adventure of discovering what God has in mind.

I first got to know Larry and Sonya when I was leading our Common Cause group ministry at Fellowship. These unique small groups of people focused their ministry on a particular cause or need they were passionate about addressing. Larry and I met twice a month along with other Common Cause leaders. We became good friends and partners for advancing God's kingdom. It was in these meetings that I learned about Larry and Sonya's entrepreneurial idea. They dreamed of hosting a five-kilometer race in Little Rock to raise money to send inner city kids to camp and to establish a scholarship fund for their education. But this isn't where they started.

Along with a small group of people passionate about this cause, they began by partnering with an established inner city ministry to children. Group members invested their time getting to know the

kids, taking them on retreats, hosting Christmas parties, producing a play with the kids making up the cast, and playing basketball. Spiritual conversations were abundant through all of these activities, and lives began to change. They even sponsored car washes, working with the children to raise money for camp. In the first year, twenty children were scholarshiped to attend the Kids Across America Kamp in Branson, Missouri. Everyone was overwhelmed by the impact of the camp experience. "Gang members were saved and lives were transformed," says Larry.

Nine years ago, Larry and Sonya's small group sponsored their first 5K race. People in the community responded favorably to the idea. A local radio personality donated his time, corporations gave money, and an African American choir sang during the race alongside the Arkansas River. Larry and Sonya's dream was becoming a reality. Forty more young people were scholarshiped to summer camp from the money raised that year, and a first deposit of $22,000 was made to an educational fund. But the adventure had just begun. As the apostle Paul writes, "Now to Him who is able to do far more abundantly beyond all that we ask or think, according to the power that works within us, to Him be the glory" (Eph. 3:20–21).

Larry and Sonya's Dream

Since that first race, God has used this entrepreneurial ministry endeavor to raise more than $1.25 million, send eleven hundred inner city children to camp, and grant fifty college and vocational scholarships. Beyond their initial vision, they also were able to send fifty more children to private Christian schools. Conservatively, 30 percent of the kids sent to camp came to know Jesus Christ personally. I'm so thankful that the leadership of our church flexed with this Halftimer's out-of-the-box idea.

On another front, God put into my wife's heart an innovative idea targeted at addressing the needs of a completely different group.

After being a schoolteacher, church planter, mentor to women, mother of three (now adult) children, and pastor's wife for thirty-five years, Carolyn found herself in Halftime. Her nest was empty. Her identity was changing. She wanted to be used by God to influence others spiritually but wondered how to go about it.

This is when the Lord gave her an entrepreneurial ministry idea. Working closely with church leaders, Carolyn secured a date on the church calendar for a four-day cruise to Cozumel for women, with a focus on relationship-building, spiritual growth, and fun. She assembled a fabulous leadership team, delegated responsibilities for various organizational tasks, and scheduled a single announcement to be delivered in a worship service.

Within two weeks of that announcement, nearly two hundred women were signed up and ready to set sail! This was twice as many as Carolyn had originally envisioned. Other women were recruited to be in charge of entertainment, still others to create gifts for each participant on boarding day. The "Sisters at Sea" cruise was an overwhelming success. God used Carolyn's teaching about pursuing God's wisdom, developing meaningful relationships, and following Christ in a powerful way. During a sharing session at the conclusion of the cruise, there wasn't a dry eye in the group. New friendships were formed, lives were changed spiritually, and loving memories were established for a lifetime. And these results put a huge smile

across my wife's face and heart. Her partnership with others using their gifts and abilities had born eternal fruit. No wonder Carolyn is still asked, "When does the next 'Sisters at Sea' cruise ship leave port?" Women in our church want to be on board!

Carolyn's Cruise Realized

Today, Carolyn is blessed by investing in the lives of six wonderful grandchildren. She still manages our home, social calendar, and disciples the wives of pastors in our church planting residency program. However, my guess is that there will be another cruise in her future. Flexing with the entrepreneurial idea of a Halftimer promises exciting results. Don't miss out on a single one.

Matching (Step 4) is challenging but rewarding. Select the pathway you believe holds the most promise for helping your Halftimer move from **Discovering** (Step 3) their *Core* (design strengths and abilities), to **Matching** (Step 4), to their best-fit *Context* (type of ministry, role, and environment). Go exploring together, gather and review your existing ministry opportunities, or get entrepreneurial by doing some out-of-the-box brainstorming. It may take some time, but it is time well spent.

CHAPTER 6

COACHING YOUR HALFTIME PARTNER

Vince Lombardi Jr. writes these descriptive words about his famous father's coaching style: "After telling his players what he expected of them and giving them the tools to do it, Lombardi got out of their way."[15] Vince Lombardi was committed to helping others be victorious on the football field, and his track record proved it.

In 1958, Lombardi became the general manager and head football coach of the NFL's perpetual losers, the Green Bay Packers. The team had only one victory the year before. However, just three short years later, on December 31, 1961, his Packers defeated the New York Giants 37-0 for the National Football League championship.

Vince had a way of helping the men he coached succeed to the utmost of their abilities. In 1967, after nine winning seasons at Green Bay, he decided to retire as head coach. Under his leadership, the Packers had collected six division titles, five NFL championships, and two Super Bowls.

Posthumously in 1971, Lombardi was inducted into the Professional Football Hall of Fame. The Super Bowl trophy was renamed in his honor the same year. Then in 2000, ESPN named him the Coach of the Century! (www.vincelombardi.com)

Similar to Lombardi, coaching your Halftime partner is about helping them be victorious at building the kingdom of God. It's

about identifying their design strengths (*Core*), getting them in the right position on the spiritual playing field (*Context*), and then cheering them on to victory.

Pastor-as-Coach

The pastor-as-coach image is not a new concept. Author, educator, philosopher, and theologian Elton Trueblood taught the pastor-as-coach decades ago. Bill Hull, in *The Disciple-Making Pastor,* writes, "The pastor-as-coach model accurately describes the pastoral task. The similarities are striking. People understand that a team's performance is linked to the quality of the coaching staff. With no major changes in personnel, a team's performance can improve. Vince Lombardi and the Packers make the point."[16]

He continues, "The pastor is a player-coach; he never stops playing entirely. He discovers the vast potential inherent in regenerate people. He views people as gifts from the Holy Spirit to his church. The pastor-as-coach is in the business of opening packages and taking out the gifts. Then he encourages people to grow and develop."

Jesus calls this *servant leadership.* "You know that the rulers of the Gentiles lord it over them, and their great men exercise authority over them. It is not this way among you, but whoever wishes to become great among you shall be your servant, and whoever wishes to be first among you shall be your slave; just as the Son of Man did not come to be served, but to serve, and to give His life a ransom for many" (Matt. 20:25–28).

The Chief Shepherd coaches us to win in life every day. Undershepherds ought to follow his example and do the same for others.

We are on our fifth step in the Shared Ministry Model,

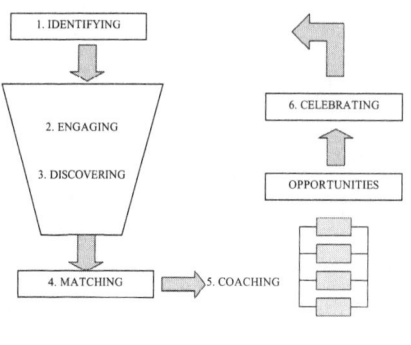

called **Coaching.** There are three primary roles that you will play as coach to a Halftimer: encourager, navigator, and pastor. Let's take a closer look at the specifics of each role.

Three Coaching Roles

Encourager Role

You cheer for a Halftimer to win at doing the "good works" God has called them to do.

It is what Barnabas, the son of encouragement, did for Saul when he came to Jerusalem after his Damascus Road transformation and tried to join the disciples. Observe his encouragement recounted in Acts 9:26–27: "They were all afraid of him, not believing that he was a disciple. But Barnabas took hold of him and brought him to the apostles and described to them how he had seen the Lord on the road, and that He had talked to him, and how at Damascus he had spoken out boldly in the name of Jesus."

Barnabas stood up for Saul. He believed in his unique calling and cheered him on to victory. The rest is history; a first-half persecutor of the church became a second-half presenter of the gospel and writer of most of the New Testament.

The wisdom of the book of Proverbs repeatedly proclaims the importance of the encourager role, as in these examples:

- Proverbs 12:25—"Anxiety in a man's heart weighs it down, but a good word makes it glad."
- Proverbs 15:23—"A man has joy in an apt answer, and how delightful is a timely word!"

It was a little after eight in the morning. I was praying as I drove to my office when the Lord reminded me that one of my Halftime partners, Barry, was launching another Life Skills class that same morning at the University of Arkansas Medical School. (You met Barry in chap. 3.) Hoping to catch him before the class started, I called Barry on my cell phone. He answered in muffled tones. The Life Skills class was just getting underway, so he stepped outside

the room to take my call. I apologized for interrupting but told him that I was praying for his ministry, that I knew God was going to use him in a special way in the lives of the students, and that I wanted to have lunch with him in a week or so to hear all about it. Because he needed to get back to his meeting, my phone call couldn't have taken more than two minutes of my time. I thanked the Lord again for our partnership as I pulled into the parking lot of my office.

"Coincidentally," I bumped into Barry's wife Lynda the following day. The first words out of her mouth were how thrilled and encouraged Barry had been by my two-minute phone call. As Lynda shared this with me, the words from Proverbs rang in my ears: "How delightful is a timely word." It felt like the Lord was speaking into my soul with a megaphone, reminding me as a coach that every Halftimer needs someone to cheer for them to win in their ministry endeavors.

A phone call, an e-mail, a written note, or joining a meeting your Halftime partner is leading are all great ways to be their Barnabas.

Tad, chairman and CEO of a successful insurance company, and I have become wonderful friends in the last two years. He was in my Halftime discipleship group a couple of years ago, and we have been processing his journey together ever since.

He called me a month ago to see if I could attend a meeting with him and two other Halftimers, Mickey and Steve. By the way, Tad leads a small group in our church, Mickey oversees ushering on Sunday morning, and Steve is helping to lead our church's relief effort to the victims of Hurricane Katrina. Tad said the three of them had a ministry idea they wanted to discuss.

All three are entrepreneurial leaders of their companies, so I knew this would be a blast. As we met over lunch in the boardroom of Steve's office, they shared their idea of beginning a marketplace mentoring ministry to young entrepreneurial leaders. In a round-table setting, with a dozen men, they want to share lessons God has taught them from failure and success about corporate leadership,

balancing family, work, and church involvement, and being a faithful witness for Christ in the marketplace. They want to cultivate an interactive question-and-answer environment to help others succeed in life, not just in business.

Initially, all three men seemed both excited and cautious. It was as if they were nonverbally asking, "Is this a good idea?" "Will this work?" Tad, Mickey, and Steve needed a coach to say, "Go for it! I believe in you! This is awesome! You are the right men for the task at hand!" It was easy and fulfilling to my own heart to say all of these things and more. These words and the conviction behind them brought smiles of confidence to their faces. I could not imagine a young businessman turning down the invitation to spend time with these seasoned leaders.

Tad (second from right) with KingdomCorp Team

By the end of this meeting, we agreed to each identify three or four potential candidates to invite to be part of a focus group to discuss the real needs these men are experiencing in their lives.

At a follow-up lunch appointment I attended at Mickey's office, we assembled our list of candidates and, in a series of e-mails that followed, named the ministry KingdomCorp. What a great name! I

attended these meetings to encourage *them,* but *my* heart is the one that is soaring over the possibilities for spiritual transformation that I believe will take place through this new ministry. I can hardly wait to watch God work through these men's lives.

Later, Tad told me privately, "I have prayed and talked with you for two years about how God wanted to use me in my second half. I'm absolutely certain this is it." Praise the Lord! Halftimers need a coach who cheers for them to win at doing the "good works" God has called them to do.

Navigator Role

You anticipate the questions a Halftimer will need answered to be able to get things done through the church.

In chapter 7 of Lloyd's reverse side of this book, he identifies a number of these questions for a Halftimer to discuss with their pastor-coach. As navigator, there are five areas where you will need to chart a clear course for your Halftime partner. These are listed below with some of the questions that will need answering.

Role Clarity: Who will the Halftimer report to and work closely with? Who do they talk to when they get stuck? Is there administrative support available to them if needed? How many hours a week are they committed to investing? (**Capacity**) Is this a paid or non-paid position?

Work Space: Will a work space at the church be needed to lead this ministry? Is there a periodic need for a meeting room at the church to conduct this ministry?

Communication Process: How will this ministry be made known to others (bulletin, Web site, e-mail, letter, video announcement at church)? What is the scheduling and approval process for church communication? Who will introduce the Halftimer and their ministry to the staff team?

Operational Matters: How does a Halftimer access supplies, a computer, phone, copier, etc.? How does the budget approval process work, and what financial resources will be available to them?

Desired Ministry Results: Who? what? and by when? questions need to be answered. Who will be involved? What needs are they seeking to meet for the Lord? In what time frame are they wanting to accomplish this ministry?

When I invited Mike (chap. 2) to be in charge of overseeing the day-to-day construction of our administration building, it was necessary for me to answer many of these questions so that he wouldn't get frustrated trying to accomplish his ministry. We had a conversation at the very beginning of our partnership about what Mike needed from me to be effective in his work. He responded, "I work best with clear expectations, direction about the priority of my assignments, and when they are due. Then I like to go get my work done, making regular reports about the progress being made. I don't like my boss overinvolved in all the details or how I go about getting things done." A healthy and honest conversation followed, resulting in one of the best partnerships I have ever experienced.

The expectations of his role were thoroughly discussed. Mike was provided a cell phone and a computer for communication purposes throughout the project. He chose to work out of his home office for this ministry assignment. This was not a salaried position. This was a high-capacity leader with a proven track record making an immense contribution to his church that he loved. As I said earlier, Mike completed this $3.5 million construction project on time and within the budget guidelines given to him. More importantly, he was allowed to glorify God by using the abilities that his Creator gave him. I could never thank him enough for his partnership in this project.

As pastor-coach, I navigated a similar series of questions with Linda (chap. 2) when she joined our staff in a part-time, paid position to direct our ministry to women in Halftime. Linda agreed to work twenty hours a week for ten months of the year. I know for a fact that she gives her church much more time and energy than this. Linda has a close working relationship on staff with Stacey, our women's ministries director.

Linda's new role was a natural because she was already involved in leadership in this area. This new ministry has been promoted through women's ministries and to the church in a worship service in which Linda was interviewed by a pastor as part of his sermon message. Working out of our church administration building, Linda has her own workstation, phone, computer, approved budget for her ministry, and access codes to printers and the building security system. She is teaching both an evening and a morning class every week called "Woman on a Mission" and meeting with women one-to-one whenever she can. She is loved, and God is using her to change lives.

I have a pre-scheduled monthly meeting with her and Tom (chap. 1) to cheer for their progress and to answer any additional questions they might have. What both of these Halftimers are modeling to others about servanthood blesses my soul.

Halftimers need a pastor-coach who helps them navigate these issues. In my experience, I have found that once a Halftimer is clear about how to get things done in their church, they require very little of my time and are incredibly productive in bearing fruit for God.

Pastor Role

You watch out for the spiritual life of your Halftime partner.

The apostle Peter exhorts church leaders to "shepherd the flock of God among you, exercising oversight not under compulsion, but voluntarily, according to the will of God; and not for sordid gain, but with eagerness; nor yet as lording it over those allotted to your charge, but proving to be examples to the flock. And when the Chief Shepherd appears, you will receive the unfading crown of glory" (1 Pet. 5:2–4).

Being a pastor and church leader, these words get my attention. Both the privilege and responsibility for being an example of Christlikeness to others and shepherding or guiding the lives of others can feel overwhelming. But this is God's calling for our lives.

Oftentimes, after a Halftimer discovers their design strengths and finds a best-fit serving opportunity, they think their Halftime journey is over. Nothing could be further from the truth. In fact, they can become so excited that they overcommit themselves to ministry, neglecting their vocation, family responsibilities, and their personal walk with God. This is where your coaching role as pastor watching out for their spiritual lives is most critical. Halftime is not just about doing some*thing* for God, as valuable as this is, but it is also about becoming some*one* for God. Both doing and being need spiritual coaching.

Earlier, in chapter 2, I mentioned two tracks in the Halftime process, the Head Journey and the Heart Journey. The Head Journey involves reassessing the course of your life and choosing to reinvest it in a best-fit serving role that you discover. On the other hand, the Heart Journey involves what the Lord wants to do in the soul of your Halftimer. It's about heart transformation, ongoing spiritual growth, and new God-given perspectives re-defining the meaning of success and significance in their lives.

It is so easy for any of us to focus on being industrious for God (doing) and neglect intimacy with God (being.) This reminds me of the words the Lord said to the church at Ephesus in the book of Revelation: "I know your deeds and your toil and perseverance, and that you cannot tolerate evil men, and you put to the test those who call themselves apostles, and they are not, and you found them to be false; and you have perseverance and have endured for My name's sake, and have not grown weary. But I have this against you, that you have left your first love. Therefore remember from where you have fallen, and repent and do the deeds you did at first; or else I am coming to you and will remove your lampstand out of its place—unless you repent" (Rev. 2:2–5).

Jesus gave the believers at Ephesus an A+ on their report card with regard to their hard work, perseverance, testing of false proph-ets, and enduring hardship. Call this an A+ in doing. He gave them an F on their report card regarding their love for their Savior. Then

he admonished them to remember, repent, and return to their first love (Jesus). As parallel tracks of a railroad are required to guide the direction of a train, so are the doing and being aspects of Halftime to guide the spiritual journey of a Halftimer.

These high-capacity ministry partners need us to help them find a healthy balance in their responsibilities at work, with family, and at church. They need us to "speak the truth in love" about spiritual blindspots that we see in their lives. Halftimers need to be coached in how to develop greater intimacy with Jesus. They need to understand that it should be a matter of concern if their heart for God is not growing or if their character and spiritual perspective about life are not becoming more Christlike. Simply stated, a Halftimer needs a coach to give them spiritual guidance.

Due to the dynamic transitions that occur in Halftime, the area of struggle that has surfaced the most has to do with self-image or identity. Many Halftimers have been defined by their careers. Others have found their identity through status symbols like titles, awards, their children's accomplishments, and appearance. Still other Halftimers have been told who they are by someone else.

In the heart aspect of their journey, your Halftime partner will need spiritual guidance as they rethink their identity, self-worth, and what is important in life.

A Far-Reaching Phone Call

I received a phone call early one Saturday morning. It was from a friend and future Halftime partner whose identity had been stripped, self-worth had been lost, and who had to recalculate what was truly important in life. Here is Brett's story in his own words.

On October 11, 2002, I was defrauded by a friend and mentor of nearly twenty years. He was a man I had known most of my life, who had given me my first job out of college, and someone I trusted implicitly. What started as a phone call on Friday afternoon escalated into a betrayal that would eventually impact many lives.

During that first night, sleep never came. My mind was racing, trying to come to grips with what was transpiring. As I attempted to think through the chaos of the last several hours, nothing made sense. My ability to think and reason, which had been my strength for years, was now trapped in a cloud of fear and betrayal. I could not reconcile what he had done with the man I believed him to be.

Somewhere in the middle of the night, amidst the chaos, I remember thinking I had to talk to my pastor and friend, Bill Wellons. All through the night, my wife Jamie and I talked and anxiously waited for morning to arrive. Around 6 a.m. or so, I couldn't wait any longer. I remember hoping that Bill would be up early on a Saturday, perhaps having a quiet time. Ultimately, however, my need to talk with him outweighed the fear that I might wake him and Carolyn.

When I called, Bill was not only awake, but more than available. When I got to his house, we began to talk and the tears came. I was scared, uncertain, and emotionally devastated. Soon, Jamie arrived and together we talked with Bill for some time. He reminded us of the faithfulness of our Savior, and that he will always be with us through any life circumstance.

Over the coming months, Bill and I met fairly often to talk. He listened, encouraged, and offered his counsel. During one of those meetings, Bill said something that caught me completely off guard. He told me that he believed that God would one day use my story to help and encourage someone else. He acknowledged that their circumstances might not be exactly the same as mine, but he believed God would use the pieces he chose. At the time, I was so overwhelmed with the pain and aftereffects of what had happened, the thought of God using me was unimaginable. But still, Bill's words were tucked in the back of my mind.

The following months and years were a struggle as I looked for work and sorted through the debris of my shattered soul. It was not easy. I went without work for nearly thirteen months while I fought the legal entanglements of the fraud. And, in the midst of all of that, Jamie developed breast cancer. At that point, I sat back and asked, "What next?" God had taken us into some very deep water, and I was not sure we would make it out. However, just when I would begin to think that all hope was lost, he would bring someone or something into our lives that would again point us to hope and a sovereign God who loved us deeply.

During this period I would often think of my life, what it had become, what we as a couple were becoming, and wonder if Bill was right. Every once in a while, I would allow myself to reflect on the possibility that God would take this mess and use it for good in my own life and possibly in the life of another.

In the fall of 2005, Bill asked me to lead a group of men who were entering what Bob Buford refers to as Halftime. I had just finished doing this in a small group with Bill. I was excited about this opportunity for ministry. It is a reflective look back at the first half of life, with the thought of redirecting our giftedness toward something of lasting and greater significance in our second half.

One day a man in my group called and asked to visit with me over coffee. We had gotten to know each other pretty well in the first few months of meeting together in our group, but I had no idea the struggles he was facing at work. He was being accused of something that he did not do, and it had the possibility of significant consequences for him professionally. As I sat there and listened to him talk about this issue and its legal entanglements, God brought to mind Bill's words of spiritual guidance nearly

two years earlier. Was this my opportunity for God to use my story to encourage this friend?

As I continued to listen, I was struck by some similarities in our experiences. I was able to recount my story to him and speak of God's faithfulness at every step, even though his hand was sometimes hidden. I was able to speak of the pain of being unjustly accused, and the fear that accompanied the possible loss of a job and reputation. But mostly, I was able to tell him with confidence that God is a God of hope and One who does not disappoint. As we left, he told me that I had been such an encouragement to him. I recounted to him the conversation I had had with Bill two years previous. He looked at me and said, "Well then, mark it down! December 2, 2005, is the day God used your story to encourage another in a mighty way."

Driving home from the meeting with my friend, I couldn't wait to call Bill to tell him that he had been right after all. God had chosen to use my story that day to encourage this brother in Christ. I was so filled with his presence that as I drove home, tears of joy filled my eyes just thinking about how grateful I was that the God of the universe would see fit to use even me.

My eyes filled with tears of sheer joy as I hung up the phone. A team member had just scored a spiritual touchdown for the kingdom, and I felt like the winning coach.

CHAPTER 7

CELEBRATING WHAT GOD ACCOMPLISHES

Put yourself in Joshua's shoes for a moment. You have been a loyal servant to Moses for forty years. Now he is about to die, and God says *you're* the man to take the reins of leadership. Suddenly you realize that your rank has changed from lieutenant to general, and you are both in charge of and responsible for the lives of approximately two million people.

God's assignment to take the Promised Land is something you were ready to do decades earlier. But as newly appointed shepherd of an entire nation, it feels weightier than before. Miraculously, you lead everyone across the Jordan River on dry ground (reminiscent of the Red Sea crossing at the outset of the Exodus) en route to your initial conquest at Jericho.

What would you do to keep your congregation focused vertically on the Lord? How would you ignite their confidence and courage? What steps would you take to remind them of the faithfulness and trustworthiness of God to use his people to accomplish what he has put before them? The Scriptures tell us that Joshua initiated a series of stone-stacking ceremonies. The one at Gilgal explains why.

> Now the people came up from the Jordan on the tenth
> of the first month and camped at Gilgal on the eastern

edge of Jericho. Those twelve stones which they had taken from the Jordan, Joshua set up at Gilgal. He said to the sons of Israel, "When your children ask their fathers in time to come, saying, 'What are these stones?' then you shall inform your children, saying, 'Israel crossed this Jordan on dry ground. For the LORD your God dried up the waters of the Jordan before you until you had crossed, just as the LORD your God had done to the Red Sea, which He dried up before us until we had crossed; that all the peoples of the earth may know that the hand of the LORD is mighty, so that you may fear the LORD your God forever.'" (Josh. 4:19–24)

Twelve memorial stones, one for each tribe, celebrating God's faithfulness. Like a mile marker, the stacked stones reminded the nation of their privileged partnership with the Lord of the universe. The monument erected at Gilgal conveyed a powerful message to everyone, "that all the peoples of the earth may know that the hand of the LORD is mighty." And that's worth celebrating!

We have arrived at the sixth and final step in the Shared Ministry Model that was first introduced in chapter 3. It's called **Celebrating.**

Celebrating what the Lord accomplishes in and through your Halftime partnership stimulates momentum for the movement in your church. It fuels vision because celebration highlights what is significant and valued spiritually, namely glorifying God through servanthood.

The apostle Paul models the importance of this for us in Acts 21. Following a challenging time of ministry, he met with the leaders of the Jerusalem church to celebrate all that God had done: "After he had greeted them, he began to relate one by one the things

which God had done among the Gentiles through his ministry. And when they heard it they began glorifying God" (Acts 21:19–20).

Luke's Legacy

At seventy-six years of age, you would think that Luke would be ready for a break in the action. But this is not the case. In every season of life, he has been a pacesetter, so why change now?

Born in 1929, Luke grew up on a farm in Oklahoma as one of eight children. True to the spirit of adventure that marks his life, he spent four years in the Navy as part of a weather squadron operating off Guam during the Korean conflict.

Following his tour of duty, Luke joined the Civil Aeronautical Administration (which later became known as the Federal Aviation Agency or FAA), where he further developed his technological skills. His career included a three-year stint in Turkey as an advisor to the Turkish Air Force and several years investigating airplane accidents as a safety inspector before retiring in 1985. Retirement didn't do much to slow him down, however. Within three years, he was partnering again with the FAA as a training consultant, commuting to Oklahoma City each week from his home in Little Rock.

You might ask yourself, "What kept someone in Little Rock when it seemed logical to relocate for such a post-retirement position?" Luke's answer is, "Because God has work for me right here at home that is far more important than any job man might offer!"

Since coming to Fellowship twenty-five years ago, this faithful servant has given himself time and again in response to a variety of ministry needs. He "hit the ground running" first as an audio operator on Sunday mornings in our worship services. When his hearing began to fail and he was unable to continue in this vital role, Luke didn't hang up his hat but rather trusted God for the next serving opportunity that fit his technical background. And he wasn't disappointed!

Luke went on short-term mission trips with our church to Haiti in 1983 and 1984. Following his retirement in 1985, he prayerfully

evaluated his full-time opportunities for service there. By faith, he took the next step and relocated to Haiti for two years. In his work with the Christian Mission of Pignon, he again utilized his first-half-of-life technical expertise and learnings to coordinate all communications and mechanical/utility systems for the mission and its hospital. He also managed a seventy-acre farm dedicated to hog repopulation in the area. Luke would tell you that relating with fellow missionaries and Haitian nationals to advance the gospel on this island nation was among "the most thrilling and fulfilling experiences of my life."

So what's a guy to do when he returns to Little Rock and the "laid back" life of a retiree? If you are Luke, you gear up for new opportunities to partner with God and your church.

After returning from the mission field, Luke responded to our church's need in the area of mechanics and maintenance on our growing church campus. When arthritis in his hands stopped him from serving in this capacity, he kept his ear to the ground for the next assignment the Lord had for him.

When the church resources ministry sent up an SOS in 1991, Luke stepped in to get things organized. Among his many achievements over the next seven years was his development of a computer program categorizing every book, audiotape, and video that the church owned. He also created a topically referenced audio-sermon

Luke Getting the Word Out

catalog of messages dating back to 1978! Tirelessly, this servant has reproduced and sent out hundreds of tapes and CDs to spread God's Word to others.

This is a marvelous legacy of service, don't you agree? From audio booth to mission field to the church facilities crew to the resource ministry—and did I mention his role as an usher on Sunday mornings for the last fifteen years?

In August 2005, we decided to stack some stones and celebrate what God had accomplished through this Halftimer. At a church-wide Leadership Launch with more than seven hundred lay leaders to start the church ministry year, we recounted Luke's service track record. Then we surprised him by calling him to the stage to receive a Lifetime Achievement Award from Fellowship Bible Church.

When Luke stood to go forward, everyone else stood as well. A standing ovation erupted and continued for several minutes. Many had tears running down their faces. Why? Because sacrificial service was on display, faithfulness over a quarter of a century was being admired, and employing one's gifts and abilities for God was being celebrated. Even after the applause died down, you could feel the spiritual energy in the room. What is significant and valued had been lifted up, validated, affirmed. God was glorified, and everyone was ready to take the land.

Venues for Celebrating

There are at least four venues in your church for celebrating what God accomplishes through your Halftimer's ministry: in a worship service, at a ministry event, with church staff, or at the board level. Here is a brief description of each one.

In a Worship Service

This venue for celebration exposes the greatest number of people to your Halftimer's story and the spiritual values you want to keep before your congregation. We call these "real moments" in the worship service at Fellowship. Practically speaking, a sermon

illustration, an on-stage interview, a personal testimony, or video presentation can be used to celebrate God's faithfulness. These "real moments" explaining how God uses "ordinary people" to do extraordinary good works are powerful stories that motivate others to want to serve in similar ways.

At a Ministry Event

This venue relates a more targeted group of people to the things God is accomplishing in and through your Halftime partnership. Luke's story is an excellent example of using a ministry event to celebrate. After all, what better place is there to uphold sacrificial service and God's faithfulness than in a ministry event for the volunteer leaders of your church?

With Church Staff

This venue allows the staff team to learn more about the benefits of a Halftimer's involvement in ministry, to cheer for your Halftime partner, and to make the Halftimer feel more a part of the ministry team of your church.

An all-staff luncheon is a perfect environment for this level of celebration. Simply introduce your Halftimer and ask them to share what God has been doing in their ministry. Allow some time for questions from other staff members and be certain to express words of encouragement for the Halftimer's contribution of time, hard work, and availability. Conclude by praying over your Halftime leader. If the Halftimer is married, be sure to invite their spouse to attend and provide something good to eat for everyone.

At the Board Level

While this venue often informs the fewest number of people about how God is using the gifts and abilities of your Halftimer, it represents quite an honor to them.

It is energizing for a deacon or elder board to hear how God is at work through the life of a church member. It adds fuel to the

vision of church leaders the same way Paul's sharing did in Acts 21 when he spoke to the leaders of the Jerusalem church.

As mentioned previously, invite the Halftimer's spouse, if married, to join the gathering of the board. Be sure to offer words of affirmation and have board members pray, giving thanks to God for the Halftimer's ministry.

Regardless of the venue you choose for the celebration, mark the moment with a meaningful symbol. Luke received an impressive etched-glass Lifetime Achievement Award. We have also used an Extra Mile Certificate, an i^2 Award, which I will describe in a moment, and a letter signed by leadership acknowledging the Halftimer's special work of service.

Don't miss out on marking the moment with a token of your appreciation. This is similar to stacking up memorial stones so "that all the peoples of the earth may know that the hand of the LORD is mighty." Marking the moment inspires the Halftimer to further service, while communicating what is important and valued to everyone involved in the celebration.

Debriefing with Your Partner

On the flip side of this book, Lloyd makes a great point that celebrating the completion of a ministry project affords a perfect time for evaluation. Debriefing with your Halftime partner at this point in their journey is healthy and will be appreciated. However, you might be wondering what should be included in this evaluation. Here are four items that will frame a simple outline for your review. You are already acquainted with the first three.

Core (your Halftimer's God-given strengths and abilities): Has the ministry project been a good fit with your partner's gifts and abilities?

Capacity (time availability for giving themselves away to others): Is the time demanded to accomplish the ministry assignment consistent with the time margin the Halftimer has been able to create? Do you sense that they are overcommitted and headed for burnout?

Context (type of ministry, role, and best-fit environment): Does your Halftimer come alive serving in the ministry in which they are involved? Is your partner energized by the role they have been playing? Are they being underutilized in their leadership skills?

Completion (desired ministry results): This is the new aspect that needs assessing with your Halftimer. Were the ministry results that were prayed for and worked toward accomplished? Were there lessons learned or insights gained about doing this ministry that require some adjustments or refinements in strategy or methods? These four ingredients—core, capacity, context, and completion— and the questions related to each one, provide you with an outline for a healthy debriefing session with your Halftime partner.

The Arts Festival

Bob was a member of one of my Kingdom Builders small groups along with four other leaders. I met regularly with them for several months processing their Halftime journeys. These early morning meetings were rich with insights shared back and forth across the conference table. As iron sharpens iron, God used these men to sharpen one another's lives.

One particular morning, I asked Bob to share his "Servants By Design™ Profile" results with us. He did, and a discussion followed where we all brainstormed and spoke into his life. By the end of our meeting, we confirmed his God-given design as a creative artist. But we had no idea how significantly God was planning to use this unique design through our church.

It started with an arts festival. Our student ministry center gymnasium had been transformed into an art museum. The decorations were fabulous. My wife Carolyn and I felt like we were in an exquisite gallery of famous paintings. Light hors d'oeuvres and punch were served at the door as we entered. It was first class! More than 125 artists statewide had created more than two hundred original works of art depicting four different aspects of the beloved twenty-third Psalm. Works on canvas, water media on paper, drawings, and

sculptures adorned the tables and wallboards forming a serpentine passageway across what used to be a basketball court. (View the art at www.mustardtreearts.com.) We were completely captivated by these beautiful works of art, as were the other fifteen hundred people who enjoyed attending our inaugural art exhibit and sale called "Exploring the Twenty-third Psalm."

Bob Hosting Arts Festival

A four-week sermon series on the Twenty-third Psalm featured selected works of art that provided visual support for spiritual lessons. Then our juror selected one piece from each of the four themes in the psalm for $1,500 purchase awards. These four prize-winning paintings are the beginning of the permanent art collection of Fellowship Bible Church.

By everyone's estimation, the arts festival had been an overwhelming success. The response from artists and visitors to our campus was extremely positive.

New relationships were starting, and a fresh connection to our state and community had begun. However, our Halftimer Bob, who provided overall leadership for the outreach in partnership with Ed, our Creative Arts Pastor, was evaluating.

Bob says, "I was the kid in the back of the classroom sketching characterizations of my English teacher." He was also the kid who grew up, received two business degrees, served in a staff position for a U.S. senator in Washington, and had a twenty-five-year career as an investment banker under his belt. In his second half of life, God is using both his artistic talent and his business savvy to launch this new ministry endeavor of our church to the arts community.

In the gap between completing the first arts festival and planning the next one, he was evaluating. Bob is energized and passionate about this ministry. It is a really good fit. And this high-capacity leader has enough vision for the future to turn his attention to this new work full-time. If he could figure out how to do this, he would. You see, Bob is confident in his heart that this is what God has called him to do.

Bob says, "With the template in place, we are now planning our second-year art festival entitled 'Beginnings' around the first three chapters of Genesis. The major change from our first year will be the inclusion of a scholars division for artists ages twelve to seventeen. Can you imagine the spiritual opportunities that will flow from hundreds of artists, young and old, reading Genesis, listening to God speak to them, and coming up with fresh visions based on these Scriptures?"

These refinements all resulted from a time of careful evaluation. Carolyn and I are looking forward to meeting these young artists and their families. We are anticipating our opportunity to connect with new faces from our community. And we are glorifying God for using a Halftimer like Bob to initiate such a significant outreach to others.

i² Award

A few pages back, I promised to tell you more about our i² service award. i² is a powerful symbol capturing the vision and values of Fellowship. It is the North Star that we keep before our congregation. More than ten years ago, God gave our leadership this con-

cept when Jesus' words in Matthew 5:16 jumped off the page and moved in our hearts. Jesus says, "Let your light shine before men in such a way that they may see your good works, and glorify your Father who is in heaven." i² stands for "*I*rresistible lifestyles and *I*nfluential works of service." We are seeking to equip every person in our church to live an i² life for Jesus Christ. And when they do, we celebrate!

Bill Smith was a stockbroker with one of the top ten firms in the United States in net capital. His institutional clients were a "who's who" of international investment management.

Outwardly, he had it all, but inwardly he was coming apart. In a testimony of his life called "Surprised," Bill wrote: "I was religious in the sense that I worshipped many gods over the years. Success, hard work, money, position, power, and the high life were my gods. They all failed to deliver where it counted, in my heart.

"Then I turned to religion and philosophy, as long as it was not Christian. I made the rounds: Buddhism, Taoism, Zen, Hinduism, and many new-age derivations. But they didn't fill the void in my heart either."

However, with some time to kill in a Salt Lake City hotel in June 1987, Bill opened the drawer of the bedside table and picked up a Gideon Bible. He turned to the Gospel of John and began reading: "In the beginning was the Word, and the Word was with God, and the Word was God. He was in the beginning with God. All things came into being by Him, and apart from Him nothing came into being that has come into being. In Him was life, and the life was the Light of men. . . . He came to His own, and those who were His own did not receive Him. But as many as received Him, to them He gave the right to become children of God, even to those who believe in His name" (John 1:1–4, 11–12).

"For the first time I felt a surprising desire to respond and move toward him," says Bill.

When he got home, Bill purchased a version of the *Living Bible* called *The One-Year Bible* to follow Jesus and his disciples through

all four Gospel accounts. Increasingly, Bill began to sense the presence of God in these morning reading times. He said, "I became acutely aware that Jesus Christ wanted to know me personally. I couldn't believe it. I didn't think God would want to have anything to do with a sinner like me!"

Jesus wanted an intimate relationship with Bill, and Bill found him irresistible. He received his Savior, and it became Bill's greatest joy and purpose in the second half of his life "to know him and to make him known."

Bill, the Halftimer, entered a partnership with Robert Lewis, one of our teaching pastors and founder of Men's Fraternity. Robert needed a high-capacity leader to host and oversee the administration of the Men's Fraternity meetings on Wednesday mornings to more than one thousand men from the community. He asked Bill to partner with him, and Bill agreed.

For seven years, he not only hosted these 6 a.m. gatherings but recruited a leadership team to oversee traffic and parking, refreshments, and technical crews. He also organized a small group system that allowed every man to be in a group to interact over the material presented on manhood.

The larger the ministry grew, the more *capacity* Bill created by cutting back on his schedule at work until he finally sold his company. Bill had discovered his calling from God, and he was passionate about it.

Bill was a close personal friend. We enjoyed many hours together praying over his business, discussing men's ministry, and duck hunting. His love for mentoring men of all ages was second to none. I know this because he began mentoring my son, Ben, at the age of eleven. Before Bill died of cancer, he had been used by God to help hundreds of men put God at the center of their lives. And today, because one pastor and one Halftimer decided to form a partnership to build God's kingdom, thousands of men's lives worldwide are being transformed by the same Men's Fraternity curriculum. (Visit www.lifeway.com for more details.)

Bill Exhorting His Men

During the course of their partnership, Robert honored Bill with our i² Service Award in a Sunday morning worship service. He marked the moment with a hexagonal crystal with i² etched into the glass. We celebrated before the congregation what is important and valued by our church, namely, glorifying God through servanthood. And because of the power of what God did in and through Bill's life, other men and women have stepped up to serve the Lord.

Men's Fraternity Graduation

In the first century of the Roman Empire, there was an undeniable social movement called "The Rise of Christianity." It was characterized by a growing *multitude* of Christians who, at a unique *moment* in time, embraced a common *mission* in search of greater *meaning* and purpose in their lives.

Secular sociologist and author Rodney Stark concludes,

Christianity revitalized life in Greco-Roman cities by providing new norms and new kinds of social relationships able to cope with many urgent urban problems.

To cities filled with the homeless and impoverished, Christians offered charity as well as hope. To cities filled with newcomers and strangers, Christianity offered an immediate basis for attachments. To cities filled with orphans and widows, Christianity provided a new and expanded sense of family. To cities torn by violent ethnic strife, Christianity offered a new basis for social solidarity [CF pelican 1987:21]. And to cities faced with epidemics, fires and earthquakes, Christianity offered effective nursing services.[17]

This shining moment in history occurred when God empowered one person, and then another and another, to live out their theology. And in so doing, he transformed not only the Roman culture but our world today.

In the twenty-first century, there is another undeniable social movement called "The Halftime Phenomenon." It is characterized by these same ingredients: a growing *multitude* of Christians who, at a unique *moment* in time, embrace a common *mission*, in search of greater *meaning* and purpose in their lives.

The invisible force behind this movement, as in the first, lies in the power of God to enable one Halftimer and then another and another to live out their theology by doing the "good works which God prepared beforehand" for them to do.

The power is the power of one person's story. The stories that result from a Halftime partnership are the kindling God supplies for you to fuel a broader vision to your church—your story, my story, Lloyd's story, and the scores of future Halftimer stories that will be ignited as pastors start building God's kingdom, through our churches, one partnership at a time.

To take your study a step further, please see page 106.

ACKNOWLEDGMENTS

Lloyd Reeb—Thank you, Lloyd, for your partnership and for representing our Savior with excellence. Your passion to help marketplace leaders have an impact for God is second to no one.

Tracy Noble—You are amazing. Thank you for your creativity and editing expertise. You made the process fun. However, even more than your work, I value your friendship.

Ann Blair—Thank you, Ann, for being my faithful associate in ministry and friend. Your insights, people skills, and organizational abilities improve everything we do.

Tom Hill and Linda Slaton—Thank you for joining me to lead the ministry to men and women in Halftime at Fellowship. Tom, you and I have enjoyed an unlimited partnership for a long time. God is using you both mightily. It is pure joy for me to co-labor with you.

Carolyn Wellons—You are a godly woman and wife. Thank you for your prayers for me, hours of listening and feedback, and constant cheerleading. You make me a better man.

Kingdom Builders—I am grateful to the Lord for the privilege I enjoy partnering with Halftimers who have become Kingdom Builders for God. My Kingdom Builder relationships at Fellowship Bible Church are among the most significant I have over the course of thirty years of ministry. Thank you for blessing my life so deeply.

NOTES

1. Will Durant, *Caesar and Christ* (New York: MJF Books, 1944), 652.

2. Rodney Stark, *The Rise of Christianity* (Princeton, N.J.: Princeton University Press, 1996), 3.

3. William H. McNeill, *Plagues and Peoples* (New York: Anchor Press/ Doubleday, 1976), 116.

4. Stark, *The Rise of Christianity*, 82.

5. Paul Johnson, *A History of Christianity* (New York: Simon & Schuster, 1976), 75.

6. Stark, *The Rise of Christianity*, 7.

7. George Barna, *The Second Coming of the Church* (Nashville: Word Publishing, 1998), 5.

8. Peter F. Drucker, "Managing Knowledge Means Managing Oneself," *Leader to Leader* 16 (Spring 2000).

9. Bob Buford, *Finishing Well: What People Who REALLY Live Do Differently!* (Brentwood, TN: Integrity Publishers, 2004), front matter.

10. MetLife Foundation/Civic Ventures "New Face of Work Study" (June 2005), 7.

11. Ibid.

12. *Reinventing Aging: Baby Boomers and Civic Engagement* (Boston: Harvard School of Public Health-MetLife Foundation, 2004), 3.

13. Charles R. Swindoll, *Moses: A Man of Selfless Dedication* (Nashville: W Publishing Group, 1999), 20.

14. Warren Bird, "High-Capacity Halftimers," *Leadership Journal* (Spring 2005).

15. Vince Lombardi Jr., *What It Takes to Be #1* (New York: McGraw-Hill, 2001), 259.

16. Bill Hull, *The Disciple-Making Pastor* (Grand Rapids: Fleming H. Revell, 2004), 91.

17. Stark, *The Rise of Christianity*, 161.